Top Down Sweaters

Knit to Fit from Top to Bottom

Doreen L. Marquart

Martingale®
& COMPANY

Top Down Sweaters:

Knit to Fit from Top to Bottom

© 2007 by Doreen L. Marquart

Martingale®
& C O M P A N Y

Martingale & Company

20205 144th Ave. NE

Woodinville, WA 98072-8478 USA

www.martingale-pub.com

Printed in China

12 11 10 09 08 07   8 7 6 5 4 3 2 1

Credits

CEO	Tom Wierzbicki
Publisher	Jane Hamada
Editorial Director	Mary V. Green
Managing Editor	Tina Cook
Technical Editor	Donna Druchunas
Copy Editor	Durby Peterson
Design Director	Stan Green
Illustrator	Robin Strobel
Cover and Text Designer	Regina Girard
Photographer	Brent Kane

Mission Statement

Dedicated to providing quality products and service to inspire creativity.

Library of Congress Cataloging-in-Publication Data

Library of Congress Control Number: 2006026572

ISBN: 978-1-56477-697-6

Dedication

To Kim Yeazel and Margo Swan. Without your continued support and dedication, this book would never have become a reality. Your willingness to work extra hours at the shop and constantly perform above and beyond the call of duty are appreciated more than words could ever say. I feel very blessed to have the two best employees any yarn-shop owner could ever ask for—and even more privileged to be able to call you my friends! Thank you for being there for me.

Acknowledgments

I'd like to thank the following:

My great customers! You are always more than willing to share you thoughts and opinions. Thank you for allowing me to share my ideas and visions with you. Your continued support and enthusiasm keeps my creativity going and on track!

All the wonderful yarn companies who furnished yarn for the garments in this book. It is great to have such fantastic fibers to work and create with.

Martingale & Company—thank you for your excellent guidance and continued support in my design work. It has been a pleasure to work with everyone involved in the production of this book.

Contents

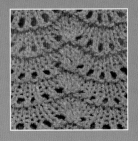

Introduction

Have you ever

- Purchased yarn for a sweater, gotten home, changed your mind about the pattern you were going to use, and then been unsure that you'd have enough yarn to complete the garment?

- Almost finished knitting an entire sweater only to realize that if you had made the body just a row or two shorter, you actually would have had enough yarn to finish the sleeves?

- Fallen in love with a sweater design but it just wasn't the right length from hem to armhole for you, so you didn't make it because you weren't quite sure how much longer you would want it?

- Wished that you could try on the sweater you were knitting before you had to make the final decision regarding the finished length?

- Been unsure of what type of bottom finishing you wanted on a sweater and wished you could try on the sweater before making a commitment?

If you answered yes to any of the above, then this is the book for you. Every design in this book is created from the top down.

Now, if "top down" makes you automatically think "raglan," then think again. I have given you several options and approaches to knitting from the top down. While you may have to think outside the box a little, I'm sure you'll find these designs a pleasure to create. So grab your needles, get some yarn, take a look at knitting from a different angle—and then *knit on down!*

Refer to the following instructions if you need help with any of the knitting techniques used in this book.

Provisional Cast On

A provisional cast on is a way to cast on using waste yarn. This technique is used when you need to work into the cast-on stitches at a later time, forming an invisible join. I use this technique on the back of many sweaters. When you are ready to knit the front of the sweater, you remove the provisional cast on and put the live stitches onto a needle.

Picking Up (or Casting On) the Stitches

Pick a piece of smooth scrap yarn and a crochet hook that is appropriate for the size yarn you are knitting with. Make a chain that contains approximately 10% more stitches than you need to cast on. (For example, if the pattern says to provisionally cast on 50 stitches, make a chain approximately 55 stitches long.) Don't worry that your chains are not perfect, because you will be ripping the chain out when assembling the sweater.

Once you have the number of chain stitches you need, cut the yarn and pull the tail through to secure. Now take a look at your chain. You'll notice that the front side has V shapes on it while the back side has horizontal bars.

With the yarn and needles required for the garment, you'll be picking up stitches through the bar on the back side of the chain. To do this easily, insert the needle from the top down into the bar, loop the working yarn around the needle, and pull through a stitch.

Don't worry if you miss a bar along the way. That's why you made the chain longer than you needed.

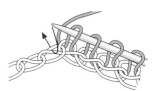

Removing the Chain

To remove the chain, take out the secured end of the chain (the end of the chain where you stopped making stitches) and place the stitches onto a knitting needle as you pull out the chain. Be extremely careful that you do not miss the first stitch—it's really more of a half stitch, but in order to maintain the same number of stitches that you originally picked up, you need to also pick up this half stitch.

To ensure that the stitches don't get twisted during the process, be sure that the right-hand side of each stitch is toward the front of the needle.

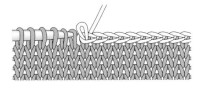

Knitted Cast On

The knitted cast on is great when you need to cast on in the middle of a garment for one reason or another. It is also useful when you need to cast on a large number of stitches (for an afghan or sweater done in the round, for example). You don't have to guesstimate the amount of yarn that will have to be left for the tail section. Some people have a tendency to make the knitted cast on too tight, so be careful of this.

Make a slipknot and place it on the needle in your left hand. Go in and knit that stitch, but *do not* take it off of either needle. Now, bring the left needle around to the front and pick up the stitch created on the right-hand needle from the bottom of the stitch and place it on the left-hand needle. Tighten slightly around the needle. Repeat this process until you reach the desired number of stitches.

Working in the Round

When working in the round, the first stitch you cast on becomes the first stitch you knit. First make sure all your cast-on stitches are facing the same direction and not twisted. Place a marker onto the right-hand needle to mark the beginning of the round. Knit the first stitch. Give this stitch a little extra tug to avoid leaving a gap. The row is now joined.

Increasing

One recommended increase for the sweaters in this book is "M1," or "make 1 stitch." When done correctly, this increase is virtually invisible.

Work up to the point where the increase is to be worked. Then pick up the horizontal bar between the stitch just worked and the next stitch by inserting the left needle from front to back and placing the new loop onto the left needle. Knit the new stitch through the back loop.

You will notice that you are actually *twisting* this stitch. That is correct. If you don't twist the stitch, you will get a hole. By knitting into the back of the stitch, you will eliminate the hole.

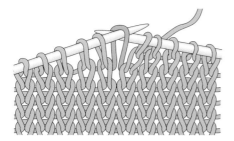

Decreasing

While there are many ways to increase, the following are the decreases I used for the sweaters in this book.

Knit Two Together (K2tog)

This is a decrease that slants toward the right. Instead of going in to knit the next stitch on the left needle, simply insert the right-hand needle from left to right through the second stitch *and* the first stitch on the left-hand needle and knit them together as one stitch.

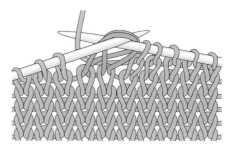

Knit Two Together through Back Loops (K2tog tbl)

This is a decrease that slants toward the left. Work up to where the decrease is to go. Then insert the needle through the back loops of the first two stitches on the left needle at once. Work the two stitches together as one stitch.

Slip, Slip, Knit (ssk)

This is a decrease that slants toward the left. Work up to where the decrease is to go. Then slip the next two stitches *individually* as if to knit onto the right-hand needle. Now insert your left-hand needle in the front part of the stitches from left to right and knit these two stitches together, making one stitch.

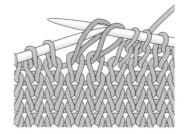 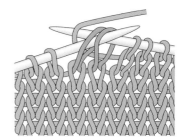

Three-Needle Bind Off

This is a very attractive bind off, and it adds stability to the shoulder area. Place the back shoulder stitches and the front shoulder stitches onto separate needles that are the same size as your project needles. Hold these needles in your left hand with right sides of the knitting together.

Taking a third needle (the same size), knit the first stitch from the front needle together with the first stitch from the back needle, ending up with one stitch on the right-hand needle. Knit the next two stitches together in the same manner, ending up with two stitches total on the right-hand needle. Now simply bring the first stitch you knit up and over the second stitch you knit.

Continue working across the row, knitting one stitch from the front together with one stitch from the back. Each time you have two stitches on the right-hand needle, bind one off. When you get down to just one stitch left, cut the yarn and pull the end through to secure the tail of the yarn.

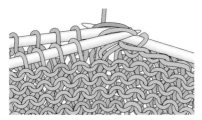

Knit together 1 stitch from front needle and 1 stitch from back.

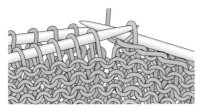

Bind off.

Picking Up Stitches

To pick up stitches for the neck band, divide the neck opening into four sections. Divide the number of stitches you have to pick up by four and pick up that number of stitches in each section.

To pick up the stitches, go under both strands of the edge stitch. If you go through only the very outside loop, you will pull the stitch out of shape and create a hole. Because the number of stitches per row is not the same as stitches per inch, you may have to make some adjustments when picking up stitches. You do not need to pick up a stitch in every space across. To avoid leaving holes, pick up stitches so that they are evenly spaced.

Should a particular stitch appear loose or leave a hole, knit this stitch through the back loop and that should take care of it!

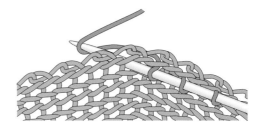

Crochet Edging

Crochet is a particularly nice way to edge knitting. It gives a finished look without adding too much length to the garment. Single crochet and reverse single crochet can be used separately as edgings. However, once reverse single crochet is done, you cannot work anything else beyond it, because you will no longer have any stitches to go into.

When using reverse single crochet to edge knitting, it is best to work a row of single crochet along the edge first so that you have a base to work from. To do this, select a hook size that is appropriate for the yarn you're working with. With the right side facing you, work a row of single crochet evenly across the edge you will be applying the border to. You may have to skip a knitted stitch here and there to make sure the work lies flat. If you need to go around a corner, simply put two or three single crochets in the very corner stitch and carry on!

Single Crochet

To single crochet, make a slipknot and place it on your hook. *Now insert your hook into the first stitch, going under two strands to prevent any holes, wrap the yarn over the crochet hook, and pull through. You should now have two loops on the hook. Wrap the yarn over the hook again and pull through both stitches on the hook, leaving one stitch on the hook. Repeat from the *, working into each stitch along the edge.

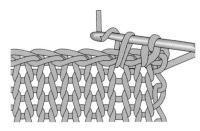

Insert hook into stitch, yarn over hook, pull loop through to front, yarn over hook.

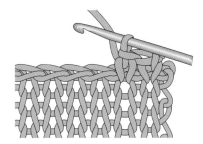

Pull loop through both loops on hook.

Reverse Single Crochet (Crab Stitch/Knurl Stitch)

After you have worked single crochet across or around the entire area you are edging, chain one but *do not turn* your work. If you are working in the round, join with a slip stitch to the first single crochet. *Remember not to turn your work.*

Now working in the opposite direction than you normally work, work a second row of single crochet over the foundation row you just made. You will notice that you have a lovely row of loops that go tightly over the top of the crocheting. If your loops are uneven, try again. This technique takes a little practice but is well worth the effort.

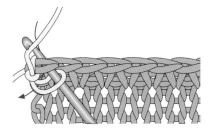

Join yarn with slip stitch. Insert hook into first stitch to the right.

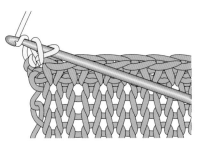

Pull loop through both loops on hook.

I-Cord

Using two double-pointed needles in the size recommended in the pattern, cast on three stitches (or whatever the pattern calls for).

Knit these three stitches. *Do not turn your work.* Place the needle with the three stitches back in your left hand and slide the stitches back to the opposite end. Knit these three stitches again, bringing the working yarn across the back of your work in order to knit the stitches. Try to keep the yarn taut as you bring it across. Repeat until the I-cord is the desired length.

You will notice after a few "rows" that you are actually knitting a tube. Don't worry if there seems to be a slight gap where you bring the yarn across the back. Pull on the I-cord when you're finished, and it will magically disappear!

When the I-cord reaches the desired length, bind off.

Attached I-Cord

After you have picked up the required number of stitches according to the pattern, cast on three stitches (or the number given in the pattern). It will be easier to use a knitted cast on (see "Knitted Cast On" on page 7), and this will give you the nicest edge.

Knit two stitches, then knit the next two stitches together (one stitch from the three that you cast on and one stitch from those to which you are applying the I-cord). *Do not turn work.* Return the three stitches back to the left-hand needle and repeat until all the stitches have been used and three stitches remain on your needle. Slide the stitches to the left-hand needle one last time and bind them off.

If you are applying the I-cord around the bottom of a sleeve or around the entire edge of a garment, sew the cast-on edge and the bind-off edge from the I-cord trim together to join.

Basic Pattern Stitches

Most of the projects in this book use these basic pattern stitches. Every knitter should memorize them.

Garter Stitch

In the round: knit one round, purl one round.

Back and forth: knit every row.

Stockinette Stitch

In the round: knit every round.

Back and forth: knit right side rows, purl wrong side rows.

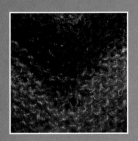

Assembly

Although there are many different methods for sewing seams, I use this method because it adds virtually no bulk. If the seam you're sewing together is a side edge, go through the very outside strand of yarn. If the seam is a bound-off edge, go through both strands of the edge stitch. *Weave back and forth* (the side where the needle comes out is the side you go into for the next stitch). This makes a nice, flat seam. Sometimes, on one side you will be working with bound-off stitches while on the other side of the seam you may have side stitches. In this case, go under the very outside strand on one piece but under both strands of the bound-off stitch on the other.

Flat Sleeve Assembly

This technique works great for sewing sleeves that were knit flat onto the body section that was also knit flat. Mark on both the front and back sections the depth of the sleeve (as given in the beginning of the pattern directions) and place a marker. Now find the center point of the sleeve and place a marker there.

Place the right side of the sleeve together with the right side of the body, matching the shoulder seam with the center sleeve marker and matching the sleeve edges with the markers you placed for sleeve depth. Pin sleeve into place.

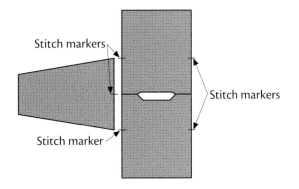

Stitch markers
Stitch markers
Stitch marker

Thread a piece of yarn (or use the tail left from the bind off of the sleeve, if you've remembered to leave one that is long enough). Attach the sleeve to the body by weaving back and forth. It works best to go through both sides of the bound-off stitch on the sleeve and the very outside loop of the stitch on the body part. This makes for a nice flat seam. Maintaining an even tension throughout is essential so your seam doesn't pucker or leave holes. You'll find that you need to go through each bind-off stitch of the sleeve but you do not have to go through every stitch on the body section. Simply line up the sleeve section and go through the stitch on the body that is directly across from it. You will be skipping only an occasional stitch on the side section.

Weaving in Ends

Weave in ends for 2" to 3" to ensure that they don't peek back out. Work down at an angle on the wrong side, going under one strand of the stitch. After about 1½", go up about the same distance in the opposite direction, forming a V. This technique holds the ends in place quite nicely.

Kitchener Stitch

The kitchener stitch is a type of grafting that is used to join two pieces of knitting together. It is done by creating a row of knitting by hand with a tapestry needle and is completely flat and invisible when complete.

Hold needles parallel, with wrong sides of the work together. Thread a piece of yarn long enough to work the number of stitches you have on the needles. (Make sure you leave enough yarn so that you don't run out partway through). Proceed as follows.

First Stitch

Front needle: Insert the tapestry needle as if to purl that stitch, leave the stitch on the knitting needle, and pull yarn through.

Back needle: Insert the tapestry needle as if to knit that stitch, leave the stitch on the knitting needle, and pull yarn through.

Remainder of Row until Last Stitch

Front needle: Insert the tapestry needle as if to knit the first stitch and slip it off onto the tapestry needle. Immediately go through the next stitch on the front needle as if to purl, leaving it on the knitting needle, and pull the yarn through both stitches.

Back needle: Insert the tapestry needle as if to purl the first stitch and slip it off the tapestry needle only. Immediately go through the next stitch on the back needle as if to knit, leaving it on the knitting needle, and pull the yarn through both stitches.

Last Stitch

Front needle: Insert the tapestry needle as if to knit the stitch and slip it off.

Back needle: Insert the tapestry needle as if to purl the stitch, slip it off, and pull through both stitches.

Weave in the yarn tail on the wrong side.

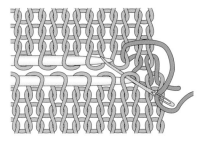

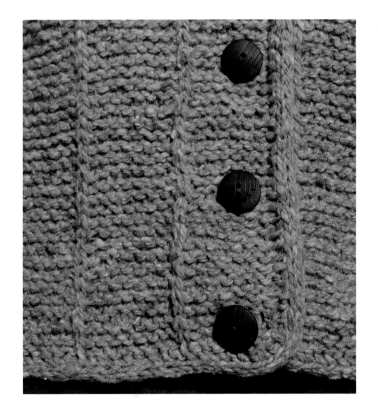

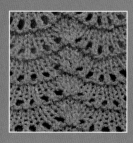

Scalloped-Lace Trimmed Sweater

Skill level: Intermediate ◼◼◼◻

Finished bust measurement: 33 (38, 43, 48, 53)"

Finished length: 19 (20, 20, 21, 21)"

Sleeve drop: 9 (9½, 10, 10½, 11)"

Materials

Yarn: 6 (7, 8, 9, 10) hanks of Silky Wool from Elsebeth Lavold (50 g; 175 m; 65% wool/35% silk) in color 07 (gold) or approx 1150 (1350, 1540, 1700, 1900) yds of DK-weight yarn 🧶

Needles: 16" and 29" size 5 circular needles or size required to obtain gauge, size 5 double-pointed needles, 29" size 6 circular needle, size 6 double-pointed needles

Notions: Stitch holders, stitch markers, scrap of smooth DK-weight yarn, size F (3.75 mm) crochet hook

Gauge

5½ sts and 7 rows = 1" in St st on size 5 needle

Back

Starting at top of back, provisionally CO 91 (104, 117, 130, 143) sts (see "Provisional Cast On" on page 7) onto 29" size 5 circular needle. Work in St st until piece measures 8 (8½, 9, 9½, 10)" from beg. Place these sts onto holders.

Front

Remove provisional CO from top of back piece and place these sts onto 29" size 5 circular needle, being careful not to lose any sts (see "Removing the Chain" on page 7)—91 (104, 117, 130, 143) sts.

Dress it up or dress it down. This sweater is equally at home with jeans or with that special outfit for a night on the town. The simple neck finish allows the scalloped lace trim on the three-quarter-length sleeves and sweater bottom to stand out.

With RS facing you, attach yarn and K31 (36, 41, 47, 53) sts; place next 29 (32, 35, 36, 37) sts onto holder to be used later for neck band; attach 2nd ball of yarn and knit rem 31 (36, 41, 47, 53) sts.

Working both sides of front AT SAME TIME, work in St st until fronts measure 3" from beg of front sections, ending with WS row.

Neck shaping: Cont in patt, inc 1 st at each neck edge on next row and every RS row for total of 7 times, ending with WS row—38 (43, 48, 54, 60) sts.

RECOMMENDED INCREASE

A make-one increase made one stitch in from the neck edge will create a virtually invisible increase. See page 8 of the technique section.

Next row: K38 (43, 48, 54, 60) sts, CO 15 (18, 21, 22, 23) sts for center front section, knit rem 38 (43, 48, 54, 60) sts—91 (104, 117, 130, 143) total sts.

Work even in St st until front measures 10 (10½, 11, 11½, 12)" from beg of front section, ending with WS row.

Fold yoke in half so bottom edges line up. Pm at each side edge at fold line to denote shoulder.

Joining Front and Back Sections

Knit across front sts, with RS facing you, knit back sts from st holders onto needle following front sts. Pm to denote beg of rnd. Remainder of body is worked in the round. Cont working in St st (knit every rnd) until body measures 5 (5½, 5, 5½, 5)" from armhole (where you joined front to back) *or* approx 5" less than desired finished length of sweater.

Scalloped Border

Switch to 29" size 6 circular needle and work border as follows:

Rnd 1: *Sl 1, K1, psso, K9, K2tog; rep from * around.

Rnd 2: Knit.

Rnd 3: *Sl I, K1, psso, K7, K2tog; rep from * around.

Rnd 4: Knit.

Rnd 5: *Sl 1, K1, psso, YO, (K1, YO) 5 times, K2tog; rep from * around.

Rnd 6: Purl.

Rep rnds 1–6 until border measures 5" or desired length, ending with rnd 6. BO in purl.

Sleeves

With RS facing you and using 16" size 5 circular needle, PU 101 (105, 111, 116, 120) sts around armhole edge beg at center of underarm section. Pm to indicate beg of rnd.

Rnds 1–3: Knit.

Rnd 4: K1, K2tog, knit to last 3 sts, ssk, K1.

Rep rnds 1–4 until 65 (65, 65, 78, 78) sts rem.

Work even until sleeve measures 11" *or* 3" less than desired finished length. Change to size 5 dpns when sts no longer fit on 16" circular needle.

Sleeve border: Switch to size 6 dpns and work scalloped border patt rows twice, ending with row 6. BO in purl.

Finishing

Neck border: With RS facing you, starting at top of left front side, and using 16" size 5 circular needle, PU 28 sts along left front neck, K15 (18, 21, 22, 23) sts from front st holder, PU 28 sts along right front neck, K29 (32, 35, 36, 37) sts from back st holder. Pm to denote beg of rnd—100 (106, 112, 114, 116) sts.

Purl 1 rnd. BO firmly in purl.

Weave in ends. For scalloped edging to look its best, block sweater.

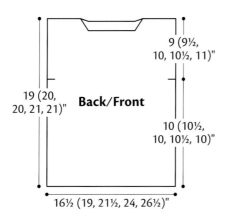

9 (9½, 10, 10½, 11)"

19 (20, 20, 21, 21)"

Back/Front

10 (10½, 10, 10½, 10)"

16½ (19, 21½, 24, 26½)"

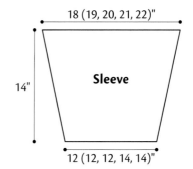

18 (19, 20, 21, 22)"

14"

Sleeve

12 (12, 12, 14, 14)"

Garter 'n' Lace Capelet

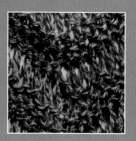

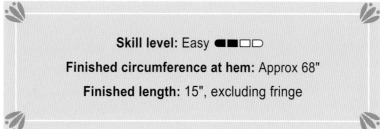

Skill level: Easy ◼◼◻◻

Finished circumference at hem: Approx 68"

Finished length: 15", excluding fringe

NOTE

The length can be altered simply by adding a repeat or two. Just remember to purchase extra yarn if you want more length. Some variance in circumference and length can be obtained through the blocking process.

Materials

Yarn: 2 skeins of Trekking XXL from Skacel Collection (2½ oz/100g; 459 yds/420 m; 75%wool/25% nylon) in color 109 (variegated purple tweed) or approx 925 yds of fingering-weight yarn 🅐1

Needles: 16" and 29" size 10 circular needles or size required to obtain gauge

Notions: 4 stitch markers (3 of the same color and 1 of different color), size E (3.5 mm) crochet hook

Gauge

3½ sts and 6 rows = 1" in garter st slightly stretched using double strand of yarn

Capelet

Beg at neck, with 16" size 10 circular needle and using 2 strands of yarn held tog, CO 24 sts, pm, CO 24 sts, pm, CO 24 sts, pm, CO 24 sts, pm of different color to denote beg of rnd—96 sts. Join, being careful not to twist.

Foundation rnd 1: K1, YO, *knit to 1 st before next marker, YO, K1, sm, K1, YO, rep from * to last st, YO, K1—104 sts.

Foundation rnd 2: Purl, working into back loop of YOs from previous row.

Yarn designed for socks doesn't necessarily have to be used just for socks!
Even the "self-striping" sock yarns have a life beyond socks
when doubled and made into this attractive, short capelet.
Wear this great accent piece with any outfit.

Begin Pattern Stitch

Rnds 1 and 3: K1, YO, *knit to 1 st before next marker, YO, K1, sm, K1, YO, rep from * to last st, YO, K1.

Rnds 2 and 4: Purl, working into back loop of YOs from previous row.

Rnd 5: Knit, wrapping yarn twice around needle for each st.

Rnd 6: Purl, dropping extra wraps from previous rnd.

Work rnds 1–6 *another* 7 times, changing to 29" size 10 circular needle when there are enough sts to do so— 232 sts.

Work rnds 1–3 once more—240 sts.

BO firmly in purl.

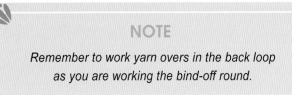

NOTE

Remember to work yarn overs in the back loop as you are working the bind-off round.

Finishing

Neck edge: With RS facing you, beg at center back, work 1 row of sc around neck edge going into each of the CO sts (see "Single Crochet" on page 10).

Fringe: Cut enough 8" pieces of yarn to add fringe to bottom edge.

Insert crochet hook through 1 st on edge of capelet and draw center of folded fringe through. Draw ends of fringe strands through folded loop and tug gently on ends to secure fringe.

Apply fringe around entire bottom edge of capelet, alternating 2 strands of yarn with 1 strand of yarn in each bound-off st. (For fuller fringe, you can put 2 strands of yarn in each bound-off st, but you may then require another skein of yarn.)

Trim fringes even. Weave in ends. Block, stretching slightly to maximize lace patterning.

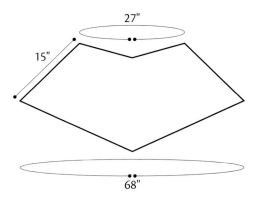

Easy Living Pullover

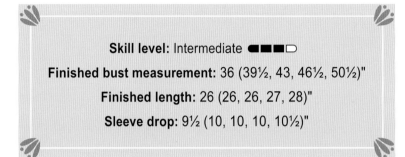

Skill level: Intermediate ◼◼◼◻

Finished bust measurement: 36 (39½, 43, 46½, 50½)"

Finished length: 26 (26, 26, 27, 28)"

Sleeve drop: 9½ (10, 10, 10, 10½)"

Materials

Yarn: 3 (3, 4, 4, 5) hanks of Texas from Interlacements (8 oz; 490 yds; 55% mohair/45% wool) in color 205 (red multicolored) or approx 1250 (1400, 1600, 1800, 2000) yds of DK-weight yarn ③

Needles: 16" and 29" size 5 circular needles or size required to obtain gauge, size 5 double-pointed needles

Notions: Stitch markers, scrap amount of DK-weight yarn, size F (3.75 mm) crochet hook

Gauge

5 sts and 7 rows = 1" in St st

Yoke

Yoke front: Starting at bottom of yoke front and using 29" size 5 circular needle, provisionally CO 90 (99, 108, 117, 126) sts (see "Provisional Cast On" on page 7).

Work in St st for 6½ (7, 7, 7½, 8)", ending with WS row.

Neck opening: K30 (34, 38, 42, 46); attach 2nd ball of yarn, BO 30 (31, 32, 33, 34) sts, K30 (34, 38, 42, 46). Working both sides AT SAME TIME with separate balls of yarn, cont working in St st as established until yoke measures 9½ (10, 10, 10½, 11)" from beg, ending with WS row.

Yoke back: K30 (34, 38, 42, 46), CO 30 (31, 32, 33, 34) sts (see "Knitted Cast On" on page 7); using same yarn, K30 (34, 38, 42, 46) from other side. Cut 2nd ball of yarn.

This sweater is one of those styles that you will want to live in. Its loose-fitting style makes it extra comfy, and the hand-painted yarn adds a dimension all its own.

Cont working in St st until yoke back measures 9½ (10, 10, 10½, 11)", ending with WS row.

Joining yoke to form body: Knit across back yoke sts, remove provisional CO from bottom of front yoke and knit these sts onto same needle as back sts, being careful not to lose any sts. (See "Removing the Chain" on page 7.) Pm to denote beg of rnd—180 (198, 216, 234, 252) total sts.

Body

Rnds 1–3, 5, and 7: Knit.

Rnds 4 and 6: Purl.

Begin Body Pattern

Rnd 1: Knit.

Rnd 2: *K6, P3, rep from * around.

Rep rnds 1 and 2 until body measures 15½ (15, 15, 15½, 16)" from joining row or 1" less than desired finish length, ending with rnd 1.

Bottom Border

Rnds 1 and 3: Purl.

Rnds 2 and 4: Knit.

BO in purl.

Sleeves

With RS facing you, using 16" size 5 circular needle and beg at the bottom of armhole, PU 95 (100, 100, 105, 110) sts around armhole opening. Pm to denote beg of rnd. Working in St st, dec 1 st at beg and end of 4th rnd and every 4th rnd thereafter until you have 45 (50, 50, 55, 60) sts. Change to dpns when sts no longer fit on 16" circular needle. Cont to work even in St st until sleeve measures 18" *or* 1" less than desired finished length.

RECOMMENDED DECREASE

To shape decs so they are mirror images, K1, K2tog at beg of rnd; ssk, K1 at end of rnd.

Sleeve Border

Rnds 1 and 3: Purl.

Rnds 2 and 4: Knit.

BO in purl.

Neck Band

With RS facing you, beg at right back edge, using 16" circular needle, PU 30 (31, 32, 33, 34) sts, PU 25 sts along right neck edge, PU 30 (31, 32, 33, 34) sts, PU 25 sts along left neck edge. Pm to denote beg of rnd—110 (112, 114, 116, 118) total sts.

Rnds 1 and 3: Purl.

Rnds 2 and 4: Knit, dec 1 st at each "corner" of neck band by K2tog (4 sts decreased).

BO in purl.

Finishing

Weave in ends. Block sweater to measurements.

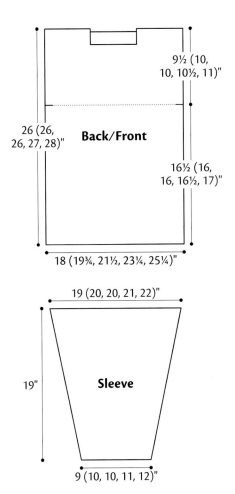

9½ (10, 10, 10½, 11)"

26 (26, 26, 27, 28)" **Back/Front**

16½ (16, 16, 16½, 17)"

18 (19¾, 21½, 23¼, 25¼)"

19 (20, 20, 21, 22)"

19" **Sleeve**

9 (10, 10, 11, 12)"

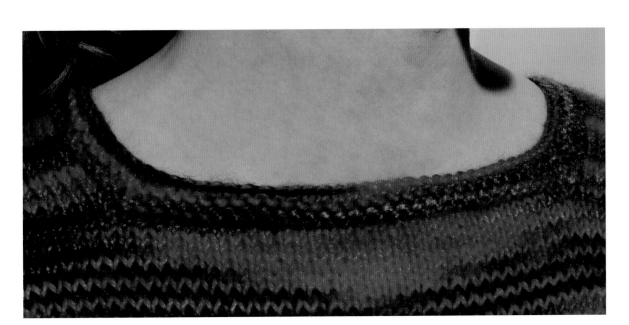

Modular Garter-Stitch Vest

Skill level: Easy ◼◼☐☐

Finished bust measurement: 36 (40, 44, 48, 52)"

Finished length: 23½ (23½, 23½, 23½, 23½)"

Armhole opening: 10 (10, 10, 10, 10)"

Materials

Yarn: 4 (4, 5, 6, 6) hanks of Roxanne's Mohair from Farmhouse Yarns (4 oz; 200 yds; 50% mohair/50% lamb's wool blend) in color Caribbean or approx 700 (800, 900, 1100, 1300) yds of worsted-weight yarn 4️⃣

Needles: 29" size 7 circular needle

Notions: Stitch holders, stitch markers, safety pin or yarn marker, spare needle in size 7, size H (5 mm) crochet hook, worsted-weight scrap yarn, 1"-diameter button, sewing needle and matching thread

Gauge

4 sts and 8 rows = 1" in garter st

Back

Using 29" size 7 circular needle and a separate piece of scrap yarn for each set of sts given, provisionally CO 48 sts, 40 sts, pm, 64 sts, pm, 40 sts, 48 sts—240 sts total (see "Provisional Cast On" on page 7).

NOTE:

You should have five separate chains that you are using for the casting on. These will be removed at different points throughout the construction of the vest as needed.

The construction of this vest certainly demonstrates thinking outside the box. Each section is joined as you go along, so there is no seaming—an added bonus!

Row 1 (RS): Knit to 2 sts before marker, K2tog tbl, sm, K2tog, knit to 2 sts before next marker, K2tog tbl, sm, K2tog, knit to end of row.

Row 2: Knit across.

Rep rows 1 and 2 until 2 sts rem between the markers, ending with WS row.

NOTE

To avoid confusion later during construction, mark the right side of the work with a safety pin or yarn marker.

Next row: Knit to 1 st before marker, K2tog tbl, K2tog, removing markers as you do these decs. *Do not finish knitting row.*

Joining center back: Sl last st from right-hand needle to left-hand needle. Turn work. Bring points of needle tog parallel with each other with RS tog. Join tog using 3-needle BO. (See "Three-Needle Bind Off" on page 9.)

Shoulder Sections

With WS facing you, remove center section of provisional CO (64 sts) and place sts onto needle, being careful not to lose any sts (see "Removing the Chain" on page 7). Attach yarn and knit across 20 sts; place next 24 sts onto st holder; attach 2nd ball of yarn and knit rem 20 sts.

Working both sides AT SAME TIME, work 10 *more* rows of garter st, ending with WS row. Cut yarns, leaving tails to weave in. Place sts onto st holders.

Right Front

With RS facing you and using provisional CO and 2 separate pieces of scrap yarn, CO 40 sts and 48 sts—88 sts total. Knit across these sts, pm, knit across 20 sts from right shoulder section; CO 12 sts at end of this row—120 sts total.

Knit 1 row even. Cont on right front as follows:

Row 1 (RS): Knit to 2 sts before marker, K2tog tbl, sm, K2tog, knit to end of row.

Row 2: Knit.

Rep rows 1 and 2 until 1 st remains on smaller side, ending with WS row.

Next row: Knit to 1 st before marker, K2tog (removing marker).

Following row: BO rem sts.

Left Front

With RS facing you, knit across 20 left shoulder sts, pm, using 2 separate ch, provisionally CO 40 sts and 48 sts —88 sts total.

Knit 1 row. CO 12 sts at end of this row. Cont working on left front as follows:

Row 1 (RS): Knit to 2 sts before marker, K2tog tbl, sm, K2tog, knit to end of row.

Row 2: Knit.

Rep rows 1 and 2 until 2 sts rem on smaller side, ending with WS row.

Next row: Ssk, knit to end.

Following row: BO rem sts.

Side Sections

With RS facing you, remove provisional CO from lower section of right side edge of back, attach yarn and knit the 48 sts. Work in garter st for 2 (4, 6, 8, 10)". Remove provisional CO from lower right front section and use 3-needle BO to join this seam.

Rep for left side section.

Finishing

Armhole trim: With RS facing you, beg at lower edge in back, remove provisional CO and K40, remove front CO and K40, PU 6 (12, 18, 24, 30) sts along bottom of armhole—86 (92, 98, 104, 110) sts.

BO in purl. Do not cut yarn. Insert crochet hook into rem loop and work 1 row of reverse sc around armhole opening (see "Reverse Single Crochet" on page 10).

Rep for 2nd armhole.

Outside edge trim: With RS facing you, beg at center back, work 1 row of reverse sc around entire outside edge of vest, working 3 sts in the corners to help them lie flat. When you get to dec line on right front, ch 8 and work 2nd sc in same space, making loop for button. Cont around outside in reverse sc to center back. Cut yarn and secure.

Weave in ends. Sew button onto left front to match up with loop location on right front. Turn down front lapels and pin before blocking. Block vest.

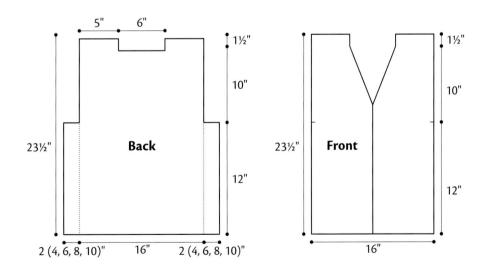

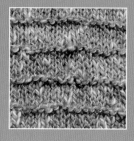

Easy Does It!
Pullover

Skill level: Intermediate ◼◼◼▢

Finished bust measurement: 36 (40, 44, 48, 52)"

Finished length: 18 (19, 20, 21, 22)"

Sleeve drop: 8 (8¾, 9½, 10, 11)"

Materials

Yarn: 3 (3, 4, 4, 5) hanks of Summer Spun from Farmhouse Yarns (4 oz; 350 yds; 34% silk/33% cotton/33% wool) in color Forest Green or approx 900 (1050, 1200, 1400, 1600) yds of DK-weight yarn ⟨3⟩

Needles: 16" and 29" size 5 circular needles or size required to obtain gauge

Notions: Stitch holders, stitch markers in various colors

Gauge

5 sts and 7 rows = 1" in St st

Yoke

Starting at neck edge and using 16" size 5 circular needle, CO 52 (58, 58, 64, 64) sts. Do not join. Yoke is worked back and forth. Change to 29" circular needle when you have ample sts to do so.

Row 1 (RS): K2 (3, 3, 4, 4), pm, K1, pm, K12 (12, 12, 12, 12) for sleeve; pm, K1, pm, K20 (24, 24, 28, 28) for back; pm, K1, pm, K12 (12, 12, 12, 12) for sleeve; pm, K1, pm, K2 (3, 3, 4, 4).

Rows 2, 4, 8, and 10: Purl.

Rows 3, 7, and 11: *Knit to 1 st before marker, inc in next st, K1, inc in next st, rep from * 3 times, knit to end of row.

NOTE

Recommended increase for this design is to knit in front and back of stitch.

The basic T-shirt styling of this top definitely makes it one you'll want in several versions. The simple patterning looks great knit in solids and tweeds as well as in variegated and hand-painted yarns.

Rows 5, 9, and 13: Inc in first st, *knit to 1 st before marker, inc in next st, K1, inc in next st, rep from * 3 times, knit to 2 sts from end of row, inc in next st, K1.

Rows 6 and 12: Knit.

Rep 14: Purl—106 (112, 112, 118, 118) sts.

Rep rows 3–9 once more—142 (148, 148, 154, 154) sts.

Do not turn work at end of last row. You will now be joining your work, so you will be working in the round from this point on.

Joining rnd: With RS facing you, knit across to first marker. Remove this marker and replace it with a marker of a different color than other markers you are using. This will be new beg of your rnd. Cont knitting around until you get to this marker again, thus completing first rnd.

> ### NOTE
> *Yes, one front side actually does have one more row than the other, but this will not be noticed.*

Cont in patt as follows:

Rnds 1, 3, and 5: K1, inc in next st, *knit to 1 st before next marker, inc in next st, K1, inc in next st, rep from * 3 times, knit to last st, inc in last st.

Rnd 2: Purl.

Rnds 4 and 6: Knit.

Rep rnds 1–6 until you have 292 (324, 340, 372, 388) sts total, divided as follows:

- **Front and back sections:** 76 (86, 90, 100, 104) sts
- **Sleeve sections:** 68 (74, 78, 84, 88) sts
- **Seam sts:** 4 (4, 4, 4, 4) sts

Body

Dividing rnd: Slip beg rnd marker, knit seam st (remove rem markers as you get to them), CO 12 (12, 18, 18, 24) sts; place next 68 (74, 78, 84, 88) sts onto st holders to be used later for sleeve; knit seam st and next 76 (86, 90, 100, 104) sts, knit seam st; CO 12 (12, 18, 18, 24) sts; place next 68 (74, 78, 84, 88) sts onto st holders for 2nd sleeve, knit seam st and rem 76 (86, 90, 100, 104) sts. Pm—180 (200, 220, 240, 260) body sts.

Work even in patt as established, omitting the incs, until body measures 17 (18, 19, 20, 21)" from shoulder *or* 1" less than desired length.

Bottom Border

Rnds 1, 3, and 5: Purl.

Rnds 2 and 4: Knit.

BO in purl.

Sleeves

With RS facing you, knit 68 (74, 78, 84, 88) sts from one sleeve onto 16" circular needle. PU 12 sts along CO edge of underarm section of body, placing marker after 6 sts to mark new beg of rnd—80 (86, 90, 96, 100) sts.

Rnds 1, 3, 4, 5, and 6: Knit.

Rnd 2: Purl.

Work rnds 1–6 once more.

Border

Rnds 1, 3, and 5: Purl.

Rnds 2 and 4: Knit.

BO in purl.

Neck Band

Beg at center back and using 16" circular needle, PU 122 (128, 128, 134, 134) sts around neck edge. Pm to denote beg of rnd.

Rnd 1: Purl.

Rnd 2: Knit.

BO in purl.

Finishing

Weave in ends.

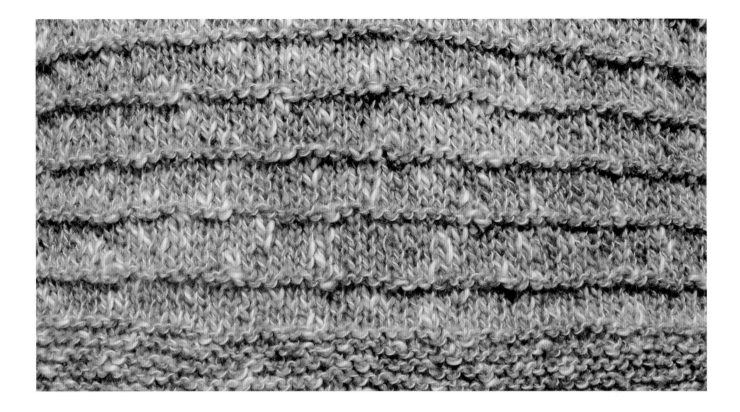

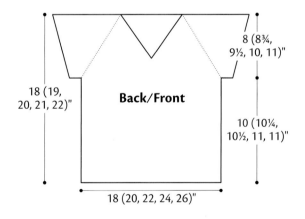

8 (8¾, 9½, 10, 11)"

18 (19, 20, 21, 22)"

Back/Front

10 (10¼, 10½, 11, 11)"

18 (20, 22, 24, 26)"

Double Play Raglan Cardigan

> **Skill level:** Intermediate ◼◼◼◻
>
> **Finished bust measurement:** 36 (40½, 45, 50, 55)"
>
> **Finished length:** 20 (21, 22, 23, 24)"
>
> **Sleeve drop:** 9 (9¾, 9¾, 10½, 11)"

Materials

Yarn: 12 (14, 16, 19, 21) hanks of Kersti from Koigu Wool Designs (50 g; 114 yds/100 m; 100% merino wool) in color 116 (greens with magenta, blue, and yellow) or approx 1360 (1575, 1800, 2075, 2375) yds of DK-weight yarn 🔒3🔒

Needles: 16" and 29" size 6 circular needles or size required to obtain gauge, size 6 double-pointed needles, 29" size 5 circular needle

Notions: Stitch markers; stitch holders; size G (4 mm) crochet hook; scrap of smooth DK-weight yarn; 7 buttons, ¾"-diameter; sewing needle and matching thread

Gauge

24 sts and 24 rows = 4" in patt st (rows 1 and 2 of body)

Body

Beg at neck edge, CO 126 (126, 126, 154, 154) sts onto 29" size 6 circular needle as follows: CO 8 sts, pm, CO 17 (17, 17, 24, 24) sts, pm, CO 1 st, pm, CO 17 sts, pm, CO 1 st, pm, CO 38 (38, 38, 52, 52) sts, pm, CO 1 st, pm, CO 17 sts, pm, CO 17 (17, 17, 24, 24) sts, pm, CO 1 st, pm, CO 8 sts.

Row 1 (RS): K8, sm, then

- *P3, (sl 1 as if to purl, K1, YO, psso) twice, rep from * 1 (1, 1, 2, 2) time, P3 for right front, sm, K1 for seam st, sm,

- *P3, (sl 1 as if to purl, K1, YO, psso) twice, rep from * once, P3 for sleeve, sm, K1 for seam st, sm,

- *P3 (sl 1 as if to purl, K1, YO, psso) twice, rep from * 4 (4, 4, 6, 6) times, P3 for back, sm, K1 for seam st, sm,

This is definitely not your basic raglan—but it's well worth the extra effort to knit! For a totally different but equally attractive look, try a second cardigan in a solid.

- *P3 (sl 1 as if to purl, K1, YO, psso) twice, rep from * once, P3 for sleeve, sm, K1 for seam st, sm,

- *P3 (sl 1 as if to purl, K1, YO, psso) twice, rep from * 1 (1, 1, 2, 2) time, P3 for left front, sm, K8.

Row 2: K8, purl to last 8 sts, K8.

Row 3: K8, *work in patt to seam st, M1, sm, K1, sm, M1, rep from * 3 times, K8—8 sts increased over row.

Row 4: K8, purl to last 8 sts, K8.

NOTE

Be sure to bring increased stitches into the established pattern.

Row 5: Work in patt to last 8 sts, K3, BO 2 sts, K3 (first half of buttonhole made).

Row 6: K3, CO 2 sts, K3 (buttonhole completed), patt across remainder of row.

Rep rows 3 and 4, making buttonholes every 24 (24, 26, 26, 28) rows or 12 (12, 13, 13, 14) ridges, until there are 414 (470, 526, 554, 610) sts total, divided as follows:

- **Bands:** 8 (8, 8, 8, 8) sts each

- **Front sections:** 53 (60, 67, 74, 81) sts each

- **Back section:** 110 (124, 138, 152, 166) sts

- **Sleeve sections:** 89 (103, 117, 117, 131) sts each

- **Seam sts:** 4 (4, 4, 4, 4) sts

End with WS row.

Dividing Sleeve and Body Stitches (Right Side)

Work patt across front sts, knit seam st, sl sleeve sts onto holders or yarn, knit seam st, patt across back sts, knit seam st, sl sleeve sts onto holders or yarn, knit seam st, patt across front sts.

St count after dividing row is as follows:

- **Bands:** 8 (8, 8, 8, 8) sts each

- **Body:** 236 (264, 292, 320, 348) sts

- **Sleeves:** 89 (103, 117, 117, 131) sts each

Work even in patt as established and cont placing buttonholes on appropriate rows, until 9 (9¼, 9½, 10½, 11)" from dividing row *or* 2" less than desired finished length, ending with WS row.

Bottom Border

Switch to 29" size 5 circular needle.

Row 1 (RS): K8, purl to last 8 sts, K8.

Row 2: K1, K2tog, K5, purl to last 8 sts, K5, K2tog, K1.

Row 3: K1, K2tog, K4, purl to last 7 sts, K4, K2tog, K1.

Row 4: K1, K2tog, K3, purl to last 6 sts, K3, K2tog, K1.

Row 5: K1, K2tog, K2, purl to last 5 sts, K2, K2tog, K1.

Row 6: K1, K2tog, K1, purl to last 4 sts, K1, K2tog, K1.

Row 7: K1, K2tog, purl to last 3 sts, K2tog, K1.

Row 8: K2tog, purl to last 2 sts, K2tog.

BO in purl.

Sleeves

Return one set of sleeve sts to 16" size 6 circular needle. Pm to denote beg of round.

Rnd 1: P4, *(sl 1, K1, YO, psso) twice, P3, rep from * to last st, P1.

Rnd 2: Knit.

Work in patt for 2", ending with rnd 1.

Maintaining patt as established, dec 1 st at each end of next rnd and every 8th rnd thereafter until you have 63 (63, 63, 77, 77) sts. Change to dpns when sts no longer fit on 16" circular needle.

Work even in patt until sleeve measures 18 (18, 18, 17, 17)" *or* 1" less than desired finished length, ending with rnd 2.

Next rnd: K2 tog, *K3, (K2tog) twice, rep from * around.

Sleeve Border

Rnds 1 and 3: Purl.

Rnds 2 and 4: Knit.

BO in purl.

Finishing

Collar: With RS facing you, beg at right front edge using 29" size 5 circular needle, start in from band sts and PU 84 (84, 84, 102, 102) sts. Work in garter st (knit every row) for 9 rows, ending with WS row. Change to size 6 circular needle and cont in garter st for another 10 rows.

Next row (WS): K1, K2tog, knit to last 3 sts, K2tog, K1—82 (82, 82, 100, 100) sts rem.

Work this row *another* 6 times, ending with RS row—70 (70, 70, 88, 88) sts rem.

BO on the WS and AT SAME TIME, work dec as established while binding off.

Weave in ends. Sew on buttons to correspond with buttonholes. Block.

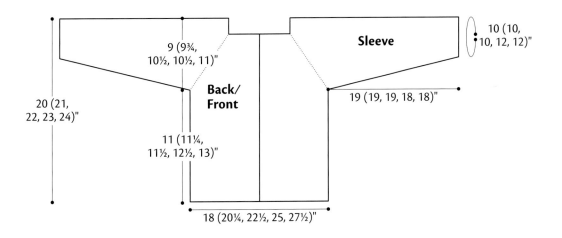

9 (9¾, 10½, 10½, 11)"

Back/ Front

Sleeve

10 (10, 10, 12, 12)"

20 (21, 22, 23, 24)"

19 (19, 19, 18, 18)"

11 (11¼, 11½, 12½, 13)"

18 (20¼, 22½, 25, 27½)"

Game Day Sweater

Skill level: Intermediate ◼◼◼◻

Finished bust measurement: 32 (37, 42½, 48, 53½)"

Finished length: 20 (22, 23, 23, 24)"

Sleeve drop: 9½ (9½, 10, 10, 10½)"

Materials

Yarn: 5 (6, 7, 8, 9) skeins of Soft Touch Yarn from Shelridge Farm (100 g; 260 m; wool/cotton blend) in color Tangerine or approx 1375 (1600, 1840, 2100, 2400) yds of DK-weight yarn ▣

Needles: Size 7 straight needles or 24" size 7 circular needle or size required to obtain gauge

Notions: Stitch holders; stitch markers; row markers or coilless safety pins; scrap of smooth DK-weight yarn; size G (4 mm) crochet hook; 3 buttons, ⅝"-diameter; sewing needle and matching thread

Gauge

4½ sts and 7 rows = 1" in garter st on size 7 needles

Back

Using size 7 straight needles or 24" size 7 circular needle, provisionally CO 72 (84, 96, 108, 120) sts (see "Provisional Cast On" on page 7).

Row 1 (RS): K4, *P4, K8, rep from * to last 8 sts, P4, K4.

Row 2: K4, *P4, K8, rep from * to last 8 sts, P4, K4.

Rep rows 1 and 2 until back measures 20 (22, 23, 23, 24)" or desired length from beg, ending with WS row. BO in patt.

Left Front

Remove provisional CO and place sts on straight needles or circular needle, being careful not to lose any sts (see "Removing the Chain" on page 7). Pm at top of each side

Knitting every row produces the garter stitch, but so does purling every row! When you put these two methods of garter stitch next to each other, you end up with garter ridges that are actually a half row off from each other. Intertwining them, which was done in this Henley-type pullover, results in an interesting design. The comfortable styling is sure to make this top one of the first you grab from your closet—definitely a cozy live-in sweater!

edge to mark top of shoulder. With WS facing you, attach yarn and work in patt across 22 (28, 34, 40, 46) sts, place center 28 sts onto st holder for neck, place rem 22 (28, 34, 40, 46) sts onto separate holder to be used later for right front.

Work 16 *more* rows in patt, ending with WS row.

Left Neck Shaping

Row 1 (RS): K1, M1, work in patt across remainder of row.

Rows 2–4: Work even in patt.

Work rows 1–4 *another* 4 times, ending with row 4—27 (33, 39, 45, 51) sts.

Left Front Placket

CO 13 sts at beg of next row. Work in patt to end of row—40 (46, 52, 58, 64) sts.

Work in patt until piece measures 5½ (5½, 6, 6½, 7)" from placket CO, ending with WS row. Cut yarn and put these sts onto spare needle.

Right Front

Return sts for right front to needle with WS facing you for first row. Work in patt for 17 rows, ending with WS row.

Right Neck Shaping

Row 1 (RS): Work in patt to 1 st from end of row, M1, K1.

Rows 2–4: Work in patt.

Work rows 1–4 *another* 4 times, ending with row 4—27 (33, 39, 45, 51) sts.

Right Front Placket and Buttonholes

Row 1 (RS): Work in patt across next row. CO 13 sts at end of row—40 (46, 52, 58, 64) sts.

Rows 2–4: Work in patt.

Row 5 (RS): Work in patt to last 5 sts, BO 2 sts, K3 (first row of buttonhole).

Row 6 (WS): K3, CO 2 sts (buttonhole completed), work in patt across remainder of row.

Cont working in patt as established, placing 2 more button-holes spaced 18 (18, 20, 22, 22) rows apart.

Work even in patt until right front section measures same as left, ending with WS row.

Joining Front Sections

Work in patt across right front side to last 8 sts. Join these last 8 sts with first 8 sts from left front side by placing right front side in front of left and doing a 3-needle BO (see "Three-Needle Bind Off" on page 9). Work remainder of row in patt.

Work even in patt until front measures same length as back, ending with WS row. BO in patt.

Sleeves

Pm 9½ (9½, 10, 10, 10½)" down from shoulder marker on each side of sweater. With RS facing you, PU 84 (84, 90, 90, 94) sts between these markers.

Row 1 (WS): K4 (4, 7, 7, 9), *P4, K8, rep from * to last 8 (8, 11, 11, 13) sts, P4, K4 (4, 7, 7, 9).

Work in patt as established, dec 1 st at each end on 7th row and every following 6th row until 42 (42, 48, 48, 48) sts rem. Work even in patt until sleeve measures 17 (17, 18, 18, 19)" from sleeve top or desired length, ending with WS row. BO in patt.

Finishing

Neck band: With RS facing you, PU 94 sts around neck edge, including 28 sts from center-back st holder.

Knit 2 rows.

BO on WS.

Sew underarm and side seams tog. Sew on buttons to correspond with buttonholes. Weave in all loose ends. Block sweater.

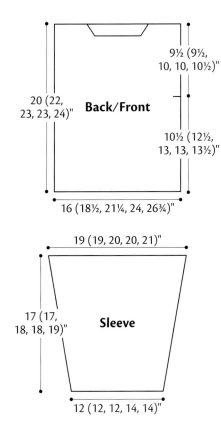

9½ (9½, 10, 10, 10½)"

20 (22, 23, 23, 24)" **Back/Front**

10½ (12½, 13, 13, 13½)"

16 (18½, 21¼, 24, 26¾)"

19 (19, 20, 20, 21)"

17 (17, 18, 18, 19)" **Sleeve**

12 (12, 12, 14, 14)"

Garter Play Cardigan

Skill level: Intermediate ◼◼◼◻

Finished bust measurement: 36 (40½, 45, 49½, 54)"

Finished length: 20 (22, 22, 23, 24)"

Sleeve drop: 9 (9½, 9½, 10, 10½)"

Materials

Yarn: 10 (12, 14, 16, 18) skeins of Kathmandu Aran from Queensland Collection (1¾ oz/50 g; 104 yds/95 m; 85% merino wool, 10% silk, 5% cashmere) in color 130 (lavender) or 1000 (1200, 1400, 1600, 1800) yds of worsted-weight yarn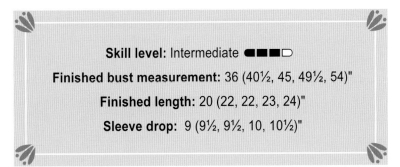

Needles: Size 7 needles or size required to obtain gauge, size 7 double-pointed needles, 29" (or longer) size 7 circular needle

Notions: Stitch holders or spare needle; stitch markers; scrap of smooth worsted-weight yarn; size G (4 mm) crochet hook; 6 buttons, ¾" to 1" in diameter; sewing needle and matching thread

Gauge

4 sts and 8 rows = 1" in garter st

Back

Using size 7 straight needles or size 7 circular needle, provisionally CO 72 (81, 90, 99, 108) sts (see "Provisional Cast On" on page 7).

Row 1 (RS): Knit.

Row 2: K4, wyif sl 1, *K8, wyif sl 1, rep from * to last 4 sts, K4.

Rep rows 1 and 2 until back measures 20 (22, 22, 23, 24)" or desired finished length. *Do not BO.* Place these sts onto holders or spare needle to be used later for attached I-cord trim.

Left Front Section

Remove provisional CO and place sts onto size 7 straight needles or circular needle, being careful not to lose any sts (see "Removing the Chain" on page 7)—72 (81, 90, 99, 108) sts. Pm at side edges to denote top of shoulders.

The loose-fitting, boxy styling of this cardigan is sure to be a winner. The attached I-cord trim adds just the right finishing touch.

With RS facing you, K24 (28, 31, 35, 40) sts and place onto st holder to be used later for right side front; K24 (25, 28, 29, 28) sts and place these onto holder to be used later for attached I-cord trim; K24 (28, 31, 35, 40) sts rem for left side front.

Maintaining patt as established on back section, work even for 3", ending with WS row.

Neck shaping: Inc 1 st at neck edge on next row and *every other* RS row for total of 6 (7, 7, 8, 8) times, ending with WS row—30 (35, 38, 43, 48) sts.

CO 10 (10, 10, 10, 10) sts at end of next RS row—40 (45, 48, 53, 58) sts.

Work even in patt until front is same length as back, ending with WS row. Cut yarn and place sts onto holders to be used later for attached I-cord trim.

Marking for buttonholes: Mark left side of sweater front for buttonhole placement. Pm for top buttonhole 6 rows (3 ridges) from top. Pm for bottom buttonhole 4 rows (2 ridges) from bottom. Pm for rem 4 buttonholes equally spaced between these first 2 markers.

Right Front Section

Return right side front sts to needle with WS facing you for first row. Beg with WS row, work even in patt as established on back section for 3", ending with WS row.

Neck shaping: Inc 1 st at neck edge of next row and every other RS row for total of 6 (7, 7, 8, 8) times—30 (35, 38, 43, 48) sts, ending with WS row.

CO 10 (10, 10, 10, 10) sts at neck edge of next RS row.

Buttonholes

Using markers placed on left front piece as guide, work buttonholes on marked rows as follows:

Row 1 (RS): Work in patt to last 5 sts, BO 2 sts, K2.

Row 2: K3, CO 2 sts, work in patt to end of row.

> **NOTE**
>
> *If the cast-on stitches for buttonholes seem a little loose when you get back to work on them, simply knit them through the back loop to tighten them up slightly.*

AT SAME TIME, work even in patt until right front section is same length as left front section, ending with WS row. Cut yarn and place sts onto holders to be used later for attached I-cord trim.

Sleeves

Measure down 9 (9½, 9½, 10, 10½)" from top of shoulder marker on both front and back sections. Place markers. With RS facing you, PU 72 (76, 76, 80, 84) sts between markers.

Row 1 (WS): K4 (6, 6, 8, 10), wyif sl 1, *K8, wyif sl 1, rep from * to last 4 (6, 6, 8, 10) sts, K4 (6, 6, 8, 10).

Row 2: Knit.

Maintaining patt as established, dec 1 st at each side on 5th row and *every 6th row* thereafter until you have 42 (42, 46, 48, 48) sts.

Work even in patt to 18" from top of sleeve or desired finished length, ending with WS row. *Do not BO.*

Attached I-cord trim for cuff: At end of last row, using size 7 dpns, CO 3 sts and work attached I-cord trim around bottom of sleeve (see "Attached I-Cord" on page 11).

Finishing

Sew underarm and side seams. Sew buttons on to correspond with buttonholes. Weave in all loose ends.

Attached I-cord trim for outside edge of sweater: Using circular needle and with RS facing you, beg at lower edge of right front, PU 60 (64, 64, 68, 72) sts along front edge; PU 34 (38, 38, 42, 42) sts along right front neck; K24 (25, 28, 29, 28) from back neck holder; PU 34 (38, 38, 42, 42) sts along left front edge; and PU 60 (64, 64, 68, 72) sts along left front edge. Cut yarn. Sl held sts from bottom edge of sweater onto same needle.

Adjust sts on circular needle so that you can start attached I-cord at center of neck back of sweater. Using size 7 dpn, CO 3 sts and work attached I-cord around entire outside of sweater. Sew ends of I-cord tog.

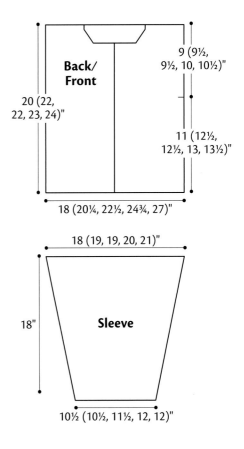

Back/Front

9 (9½, 9½, 10, 10½)"

20 (22, 22, 23, 24)"

11 (12½, 12½, 13, 13½)"

18 (20¼, 22½, 24¾, 27)"

18 (19, 19, 20, 21)"

18"

Sleeve

10½ (10½, 11½, 12, 12)"

Out-of-Shell Turtleneck

Skill level: Easy ●■□□

Finished bust measurement: 35½ (40, 44½, 49, 53½)"

Finished length: 20 (21½, 23, 23, 23½)"

Sleeve drop: 9½ (9½, 10, 10, 10½)"

Materials

Yarn

MC: 4 (5, 5, 6, 7) hanks of Cascade 220 from Cascade Yarns (3.5 oz/100 g; 220 yds; 100% Peruvian highland wool) in color 9338 (olive green) or approx 880 (1040, 1200, 1400, 1600) yds of worsted-weight yarn (4)

CC: 1 (1, 1, 2, 2) hank of Cascade 220 from Cascade Yarns (3.5 oz/100 g; 220 yds; 100% Peruvian highland wool) in color 4010 (gold) or approx 140 (170, 200, 230, 260) yds of worsted-weight yarn (4)

Needles: 16" and 29" size 7 circular needles or size required to obtain gauge, size 7 double-pointed needles

Notions: Stitch holders, stitch markers, scrap of smooth worsted-weight yarn, size G (4 mm) crochet hook

Gauge

4½ sts and 6 rows = 1" in St st

Back

Using 29" size 7 circular needle and waste yarn for provisional CO, beg at top back of neck and provisionally CO 80 (90, 100, 110, 120) sts (see "Provisional Cast On" on page 7). Using MC, work in St st until piece measures 9½ (9½, 10, 10, 10½)" from beg. Place sts onto st holders to be used later for sweater body.

Front

Remove provisional CO and place sts back onto circular needle, being careful not to lose any sts (see "Removing the Chain" on page 7). With RS facing you, attach MC

This mock turtleneck has definitely come out of its shell! The addition of a second color to accent the trim adds extra eye appeal to this otherwise basic sweater.

and K24 (29, 34, 39, 44) sts; BO 32 sts; attach 2nd ball of yarn and K24 (29, 34, 39, 44) sts. Working both sides AT SAME TIME, work even in St st for 2", ending with WS row. Inc at each side of neck edge on next row and every RS row thereafter 10 times total, ending with WS row—34 (39, 44, 49, 54) sts.

Joining Front Sections

K34 (39, 44, 49, 54) sts; CO 12 sts; working with same yarn, K34 (39, 44, 49, 54) sts from other front section. Second skein of yarn may now be cut—80 (90, 100, 110, 120) sts.

Work even until front measures same as back section, ending with WS row.

Joining Front to Back

Knit across front sts. Using same yarn, cont to knit across back sts. Pm to denote beg of round—160 (180, 200, 220, 240) sts.

Work even in St st (knit every rnd) until piece measures 5½ (7, 8, 8, 8)" from join or 5" less than desired finished length. Do not cut yarn.

Border

Rnd 1: With CC, *sl 1, K1, rep from * around.

Rnd 2: *Wyib, sl 1, P1, rep from * around.

Rnd 3: With MC, knit.

Rnd 4: Knit.

Rep rnds 1–4 for approx 5", ending with rnd 2. Cut MC. With CC, work 3 rnds in garter st (knit 1 rnd, purl 1 rnd) starting with knit rnd.

BO in purl.

Sleeves

Using 16" circular needle, with RS facing you and starting at bottom of armhole opening, PU 86 (86, 90, 90, 94) sts. Pm to denote beg of rnd.

Working in St st, dec 1 st at beg and end of every 4th rnd until you have 46 (46, 50, 50, 54) sts. Change to dpns when sts no longer fit on 16" circular needle.

Work even until sleeve measures 13" *or* 5" less than desired finished length.

Rep border as for sweater body.

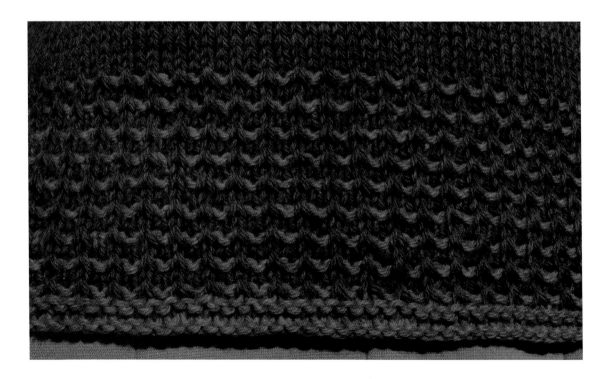

Neck Band

With RS facing you, using 16" circular needle and CC, and
starting at right back side, PU 32 sts across back, 20 sts
along left front, 12 sts across front neck, 20 sts along
right front—84 sts. Join, placing marker to denote beg
of rnd.

Rnd 1 and 3: Purl.

Rnd 2: Knit.

Rnds 4 and 5: With MC, knit.

Rnd 6: With CC, *sl 1, K1, rep from * around.

Rnd 7: With CC, *wyib sl 1, P1, rep from * around.

Work rnds 4–7 *another* 2 times.

With CC, work 3 rnds in garter st. BO in purl.

Finishing

Weave in ends. Block sweater.

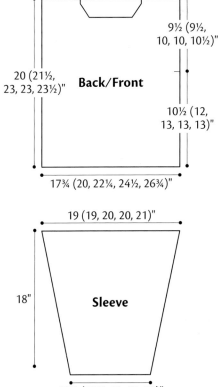

9½ (9½, 10, 10, 10½)"

20 (21½, 23, 23, 23½)"   **Back/Front**

10½ (12, 13, 13, 13)"

17¾ (20, 22¼, 24½, 26¾)"

19 (19, 20, 20, 21)"

18"   **Sleeve**

10¼ (10¼, 11, 11, 12)"

Sample-Stitch Tunic

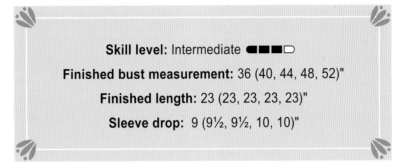

Skill level: Intermediate ◼◼◼◻

Finished bust measurement: 36 (40, 44, 48, 52)"

Finished length: 23 (23, 23, 23, 23)"

Sleeve drop: 9 (9½, 9½, 10, 10)"

Materials

Yarn: 1 (1, 2, 2, 2) cones of sport-weight Fine Wool Yarn from Marr Haven (16 oz; 1,750 yds; 100% wool) in color Light Grey or approx 1500 (1750, 2000, 2300, 2600) yds of sport-weight yarn ❷

Needles: Size 6 straight needles or circular needle or size required to obtain gauge, 16" size 6 circular needle

Notions: Stitch markers, scrap of smooth sport-weight yarn, size G (4 mm) crochet hook

Gauge

5 sts and 7 rows = 1" in St st on size 6 needles

Back

Using size 6 straight needles or circular needle, provisionally CO 90 (100, 110, 120, 130) sts (see "Provisional Cast On" on page 7).

Row 1 (RS): P3 (6, 9, 5, 8); work chart A over next 12 sts; P1, [K1, P1] 1 (2, 3, 3, 4) time; work chart B over next 9 (9, 9, 18, 18) sts; P1, K1, P1; work chart C over next 30 sts; P1, K1, P1; work chart B over next 9 (9, 9, 18, 18) sts; P1, [K1, P1] 1 (2, 3, 3, 4) time; work chart D over next 12 sts; P3 (6, 9, 5, 8).

Row 2: Purl.

Rows 3–36: Cont working charts as established.

Rows 37–72: Cont working charts as established, except work chart E in place of chart B.

Although you may find this design a little more challenging than the rest, you definitely won't get bored making it! You can easily make this tunic longer simply by adding another of any of the stitch patterns; however, be sure to do it after the armhole depth has been reached and to alter the row numbers.

Front

Remove provisional CO and place sts back onto size 6 circular needle, being careful not to lose any sts (see "Removing the Chain" on page 7)—90 (100, 110, 120, 130) sts.

Row 1 (RS): With RS facing you, attach yarn and knit across 28 (33, 37, 42, 47) sts; BO next 34 (34, 36, 36, 36) sts; attach 2nd ball of yarn and knit across rem 28 (33, 37, 42, 47) sts.

Working both sides of front AT SAME TIME, cont as follows:

Row 2: (WS) Knit.

Row 3: Knit.

Row 4: Purl.

Row 5: Knit.

Row 6: Knit.

Working both sides AT SAME TIME, work charts in same order as for back section for 3", ending with WS row.

Cont working charts as established, inc 1 st at neck edge on each side on next row and every RS row 7 times total, ending with WS row—35 (40, 44, 49, 54) sts.

Next row: Work patt across 35 (40, 44, 49, 54) sts; CO 20 (20, 22, 22, 22) sts; work patt across rem 35 (40, 44, 49, 54) sts. Cut 2nd ball of yarn.

Work remainder of front as for back.

Sleeves

Measure 9 (9½, 9½, 10, 10)" down from top of shoulder on both sides of front and back of sweater and pm at each spot.

With RS facing you, PU 90 (95, 95, 100, 100) sts between markers along one side of sweater. Knit 4 rows. Purl 1 row (WS).

Beg patt for sleeve, starting with RS row, while AT SAME TIME dec 1 st at each end of 5th row and every following 6th row until you have 50 (50, 60, 60, 60) sts.

Rows 1–24: Work chart E.

Rows 25–28: Purl.

Rows 29–64: Work chart H.

Rows 65–68: Purl.

Rows 69–102: Work chart B.

Rows 103–106: Purl.

Rows 73–79: P3 (6, 9, 5, 8), knit to last 3 (6, 9, 5, 8) sts, purl rem sts.

Row 80: Purl.

Rows 81–106: Work chart F across row.

Rows 107–111: Knit.

Row 112: Purl.

Rows 113–150: Work chart G over 15 (20, 25, 30, 35) sts; P1 (K1, P1) twice; work chart H over next 50 sts; P1 (K1, P1) twice; work chart I over rem 15 (20, 25, 30, 35) sts.

Rows 151–154: Knit.

Rows 155, 157, 159, 161, and 163: *K2, P3, K2, P2, K1, rep from * across row.

Rows 156, 158, 160, and 162: Purl.

Rows 164–167: Knit.

BO in knit on WS.

Work chart A until sleeve measures 18" *or* 1½" less than desired finished length of sleeve, ending with WS row.

Purl 4 rows.

Sleeve Border

Rows 1, 3, 5, 7, and 9 (RS): *K2, P3, K2, P2, K1, rep from * across row.

Rows 2, 4, 6, 8, and 10: Purl.

Rows 11–13: Purl.

BO in purl on RS.

Finishing

Neck band: Using 16" circular needle, with RS facing you, PU 34 (34, 36, 36, 36) sts along back neck edge, 23 sts along right front neck, 20 (20, 22, 22, 22) sts along center front edge, and 23 sts along left front neck—100 (100, 104, 104, 104) sts. Pm to denote beg of rnd.

Rnds 1 and 3: Purl.

Rnds 2 and 4: Knit.

BO in purl.

Sew underarm and side seams tog. Weave in ends. Block sweater.

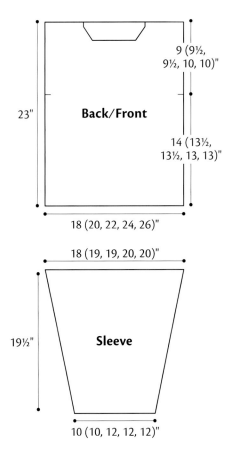

Back/Front

9 (9½, 9½, 10, 10)"

23"

14 (13½, 13½, 13, 13)"

18 (20, 22, 24, 26)"

18 (19, 19, 20, 20)"

Sleeve

19½"

10 (10, 12, 12, 12)"

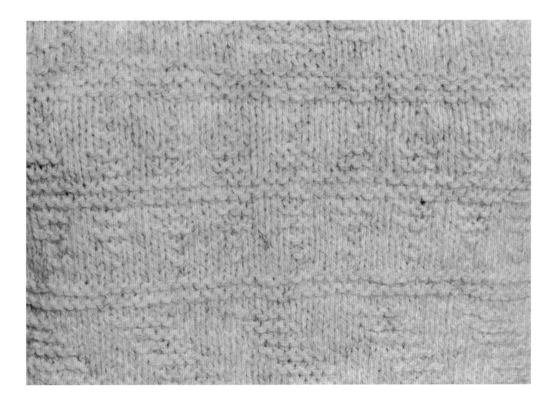

Chart B

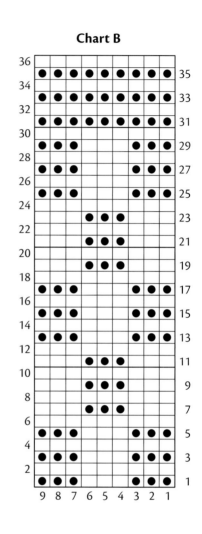

Chart A

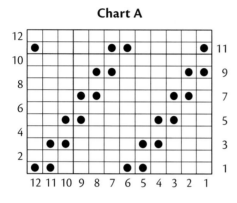

Key

☐ K on RS, P on WS
● P on WS, K on RS

Chart C

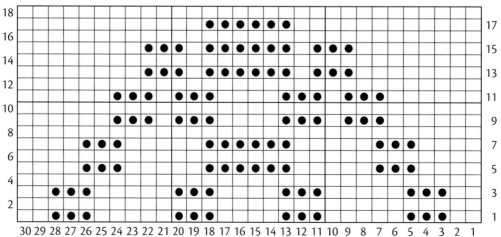

Chart D

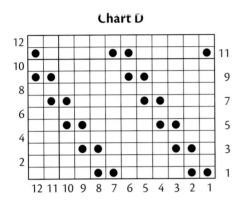

Chart E

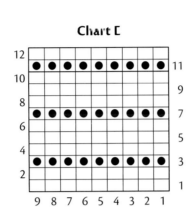

Chart F

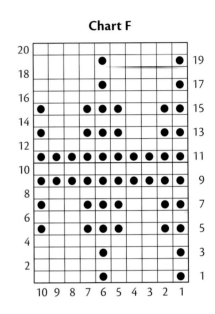

Key

K on RS, P on WS
P on WS, K on RS

Chart G

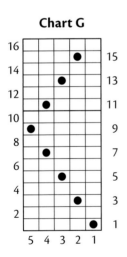

Chart H

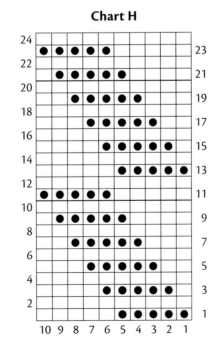

Chart I

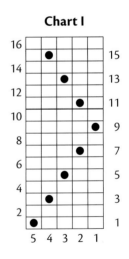

Modular Garter-Stitch Jacket

Skill level: Intermediate ■■■□

Finished bust measurement: 36 (40, 44, 48, 52, 56)"

Finished length: 26 (26½, 27, 27, 27, 27)"

Sleeve drop: 9½ (9½, 10, 10, 10½, 10½)"

Materials

Yarn

MC: 10 (12, 14, 16, 18, 20) skeins of Silk Garden from Noro Yarns (50 g; 100 m; 45% silk/45% kid mohair, 10% lamb's wool) in color 234 (multicolored) or approx 1100 (1320, 1650, 1760, 1980, 2300) yds of worsted-weight yarn ④

CC: 1 (2, 2, 2, 3, 3) skeins of Cash Iroha from Noro Yarns (40 g; 91 m; 40% silk/30% lamb's wool/20% cashmere/10% nylon) in color 95 (dark gold) or approx 100 (115, 140, 160, 200, 250) yds of worsted-weight yarn ④

Needles: 16" and 29" (or longer) size 7 circular needles or size required to obtain gauge, size 7 double-pointed needles

Notions: Stitch markers; stitch holders or scrap yarn to hold stitches; 3 buttons, 1"-diameter; sewing needle and matching thread; size 7 (4.5 mm) crochet hook

Gauge

9 sts and 18 rows = 2" in garter st

Yoke

Using the 29" circular needle and MC, CO 74 (74, 82, 82, 90, 90) sts as follows:

CO 10 (10, 12, 12, 14, 14) sts for front section, pm, CO 1 st for seam st, pm, CO 15 sts for sleeve, pm, CO 1 st for seam st, pm, CO 20 (20, 24, 24, 28, 28) sts for back, pm, CO 1 st for seam st, pm, CO 15 sts for sleeve, pm, CO 1 st for seam st, CO 10 (10, 12, 12, 14, 14) sts for front section.

Row 1 (RS): *Knit to marker, M1, K1, M1, rep from * 3 times, knit to end of row—8 sts inc, 82 (82, 90, 90, 98, 98) sts total.

Row 2: Knit.

Knitting this jacket is like building a jigsaw puzzle: start with the yoke piece, and connect and add the other sections as you go. There is absolutely nothing to be sewn together when you are finished knitting! For best results, make sure your contrasting yarn doesn't get lost in the variegation of the main-color yarn.

Rep rows 1 and 2, ending with WS row until there are 266 (266, 266, 322, 322, 322) sts total divided as follows:

- **Front sections:** 34 (34, 34, 42, 42, 42) sts each
- **Back section:** 68 (68, 68, 84, 84, 84) sts
- **Sleeve sections:** 63 (63, 63, 75, 75, 75) sts each
- **Seam sts:** 4 (4, 4, 4, 4, 4) sts

Cut MC. With CC, work rows 1 and 2 another 2 times, ending with WS row. You should now have 282 (282, 282, 338, 338, 338) sts total, divided as follows:

- **Front sections:** 36 (36, 36, 44, 44, 44) sts each
- **Back section:** 72 (72, 72, 88, 88, 88) sts
- **Sleeve sections:** 67 (67, 67, 79, 79, 79) sts each
- **Seam sts:** 4 (4, 4, 4, 4, 4) sts

Cut yarn. Divide sts onto separate holders for sleeve, back, and front sections, placing seam sts onto body sections.

Back

Using 29" circular needle and MC, provisionally CO 72 sts (see "Provisional Cast On" on page 7), pm, PU across 74 (74, 74, 90, 90, 90) sts of back section (this number includes 2 seam sts), pm, provisionally CO an additional 72 sts—218 (218, 218, 234, 234, 234) sts total. Knit back across all sts.

Row 1 (RS): Knit to 2 sts before marker, K2tog twice, knit to 2 sts before next marker, K2tog twice, knit to end of row.

Row 2: Knit.

Rep rows 1 and 2 until 2 sts rem between markers, ending with WS row.

Next row: Knit to 1 st before marker, K2tog twice (removing markers to do so). *Do not knit to end of row.* Return last st on right needle to left needle.

Fold work with RS tog and needles parallel to each other. Join center back seam using 3-needle BO (see "Three-Needle Bind Off" on page 9).

Left Front

With RS facing you, using 29" circular needle and MC, knit across 37 (37, 37, 45, 45, 45) left front yoke sts (this number includes 1 seam st), pm, provisionally CO an additional 72 sts—109 (109, 109, 117, 117, 117). Knit back across all sts.

Row 1 (RS): Knit to 2 sts before marker, K2tog twice, knit to end of row.

Row 2: Knit.

Rep rows 1 and 2 until 1 st remains on yoke section, ending with WS row.

Next row (RS): Knit to last 2 sts, K2tog (removing marker to do so).

BO on WS.

Left front band: With RS facing you and using CC, PU 96 (96, 96, 102, 102, 102) sts along left front. Knit 4 rows, ending with RS row.

BO in knit on WS.

Right Front

Using 29" circular needle and MC, provisionally CO 72 sts, pm. With RS facing you, knit across 37 (37, 37, 45, 45, 45) right front yoke sts, joining it to CO edge—109 (109, 109, 117, 117, 117) sts total. Knit back across all sts.

Row 1 (RS): Knit to 2 sts before marker, K2tog twice, knit to end of row.

Row 2: Knit.

Rep rows 1 and 2 until 1 st remains on yoke section, ending with WS row.

Next row: K to last 2 sts, K2tog (removing marker to do so).

BO on WS.

Right front band: With RS facing you and using CC, PU 96 (96, 96, 102, 102, 102) sts from right front section. Mark for buttonholes, placing first buttonhole 2 sts down from top of neck, 1 buttonhole over CC yoke color rows, and center buttonhole equally spaced between top and bottom buttonholes.

Row 1 (WS): Knit.

Row 2 (RS): Knit to first marker, BO 2 sts, knit to second marker, BO 2 sts, knit to last marker, BO 2 sts, knit last st.

Row 3: K1, CO 2 sts, knit to next buttonhole space, CO 2 sts, knit to next buttonhole space, CO 2 sts, knit to end of row.

Row 4: Knit across, working the sts that you CO in previous row tbl to keep them tight.

BO in knit on WS.

Side Sections and Sleeve Caps

Remove provisional CO edge and replace sts for one side section onto 29" circular needle. Be careful not to lose any sts (see "Removing the Chain" on page 7). With RS facing you for first row, attach MC and beg as follows:

Row 1: Knit 72 sts, pm, K67 (67, 67, 79, 79, 79) sts, pm, knit rem 72 sts—211 (211, 211, 223, 223, 223) sts total.

Knit even for 1 (2, 3, 2, 3, 4)", ending with WS row.

Joining side seam: Bring front and back sides tog with RS tog. Work 3-needle BO across 63 (63, 60, 66, 63, 63) sts, leaving 1 st on right-hand needle. *Do not cut yarn.* Turn knitting so RS is facing you again and work sleeves.

Sleeves

Place st left from 3-needle BO of side seam onto 16" circular needle and knit sts from sleeve section of yoke piece onto this needle. Pm to denote beg of rnd—85 (85, 91, 91, 97, 97) sts.

Purl 1 rnd.

Beg working in garter st (knit 1 rnd, purl 1 rnd). Dec 1 st at beg and end of next rnd and every 6th rnd thereafter until you have 45 (45, 51, 51, 55, 55) sts. Change to dpns when sts no longer fit on 16" circular needle.

Work even until sleeve measures 18" *or* 1" less than desired finished length, ending with purl rnd. Switch to CC and work an additional 5 rnds in garter st. BO in purl.

Finishing

Neck band: With RS facing you and 16" circular needle, PU 80 (80, 88, 88, 96, 96) sts around neck of sweater, starting at right edge of neck band.

Rows 1 and 3 (WS): Knit.

Row 2: K12 (12, 14, 14, 16, 16), K2tog twice, K11, K2tog twice, K18 (18, 22, 22, 26, 26), K2tog twice, K11, K2tog twice, K12 (12, 14, 14, 16, 16).

Row 4: K11 (11, 13, 13, 15, 15), K2tog twice, K9, K2tog twice, K16 (16, 20, 20, 24, 24), K2tog twice, K9, K2tog twice, K11 (11, 13, 13, 15, 15).

BO in knit.

Bottom border: With RS facing you and using 29" circular needle, PU 162 (180, 198, 216, 234, 252) sts around bottom edge of sweater.

Knit 2 rows.

BO in knit on WS.

Sew on buttons. Weave in ends. Block sweater.

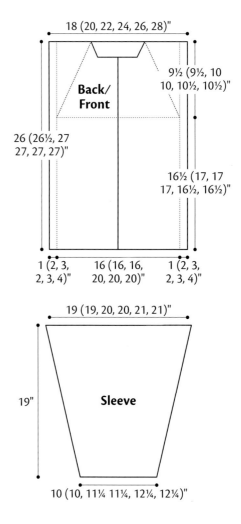

18 (20, 22, 24, 26, 28)"

Back/Front

9½ (9½, 10 10, 10½, 10½)"

26 (26½, 27 27, 27, 27)"

16½ (17, 17 17, 16½, 16½)"

1 (2, 3, 2, 3, 4)" 16 (16, 16, 20, 20, 20)" 1 (2, 3, 2, 3, 4)"

19 (19, 20, 20, 21, 21)"

19"

Sleeve

10 (10, 11¼ 11¼, 12¼, 12¼)"

Loose-Knit Cover-Up

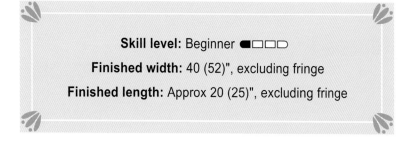

Skill level: Beginner ■□□□

Finished width: 40 (52)", excluding fringe

Finished length: Approx 20 (25)", excluding fringe

Materials

Yarn: 3(4) hanks of Harmony from Wool in the Woods (200 yds;
136 g; 48% kid mohair/26% wool/17% silk/9% nylon) in color Majestic Ridge or approx 600 (800) yds of worsted-weight yarn (④)

Needles: 29" size 11 circular needle or size required to obtain gauge

Notions: Stitch markers, scrap of smooth worsted-weight yarn, size H (5 mm) crochet hook

Gauge

2½ sts and 4 rows = 1" in garter st slightly stretched

Front

Using 29" size 11 circular needle and beg at shoulder, provisionally CO 100 (130) sts, placing marker after first 4 sts and before last 4 sts (see "Provisional Cast On" on page 7). Work in garter st (knit every row) until piece measures 5" from beg, ending with WS row. Beg dec shaping as follows:

Row 1 (RS): K4, sm, K2tog, knit to end of row.

Rep row 1 until 25 sts rem *between* markers, ending by working WS row.

BO as follows: K4, BO 25 sts. Cut yarn and secure it in last st.

Drop rem 4 sts from each end off needle. Leave these for now. They will be pulled out later for fringe.

Large needles, a textured yarn, and an easy technique that allows you to "fringe as you go" all make this a quick-knit cover-up that looks great over a turtleneck as well as a camisole. You'll want several!

Back

Remove provisional CO and place sts back onto circular needle, being careful not to lose any sts (see "Removing the Chain" on page 7). With RS facing you, attach yarn and K30 (45), BO next 40 sts, K30 (45).

Next row (WS): K4, pm, K26 (41), CO 40 sts, K26 (41), pm, K4.

Work in garter st for 5", ending with WS row. Work dec shaping as for back.

Fringe: Unravel 4 sts from sides of each piece, starting from BO edge up to CO edge.

Cut 10" pieces of yarn. Place fringe in every other st across bound-off edge as follows: Insert crochet hook through st on bound-off edge and draw center of folded fringe through. Draw ends of fringe strands through folded loop and tug gently on ends to secure fringe.

Cut loop of each self-made fringe, and then make loop knot at end nearest knitting. Trim fringes even.

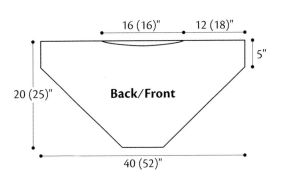

16 (16)"   12 (18)"

5"

20 (25)"   **Back/Front**

40 (52)"

Checkerboard Tweed Pullover

Skill level: Easy ◼◼☐☐

Finished bust measurement: 37 (43, 48, 53)"

Finished length: 23 (24, 24, 25)"

Sleeve drop: 9½ (10, 10½, 11)"

Materials

Yarn: 5 (6, 7, 8) skeins of Tweed Cascade 220 from Cascade Yarns (3.5 oz/100 g; 220 yds; 90% Peruvian highland wool/10% Donnegal tweed) in color 7621 (dusty mauve) or approx 1100 (1320, 1540, 1760) yds of worsted-weight yarn (4)

Needles: 16" and 24" size 7 circular needle or size required to obtain gauge, size 7 double-pointed needles, 16" size 6 circular needle, size 6 double-pointed needles

Notions: Stitch holder or spare needle, stitch markers, scrap of smooth worsted-weight yarn, size G (4 mm) crochet hook

Gauge

4½ sts and 6 rows = 1" in St st

Back

Using 24" size 7 circular needle and beg at top of back, provisionally CO 84 (96, 108, 120) sts (see "Provisional Cast On" on page 7).

Row 1 (RS): Knit.

Row 2 and all even-numbered rows through 16 (WS): Purl.

Rows 3, 5, and 7: *P6, K6, rep from * across row.

Row 9: Knit.

Rows 11, 13, and 15: *K6, P6, rep from * across row.

Rep rows 1–16 until back measures 9½ (10, 10½, 11)" from beg. Place sts onto st holder or spare needle.

Front

Remove provisional CO and place sts onto 24" size 7 circular needle, being careful not to lose any sts (see "Removing the Chain" on page 7)—84 (96, 108, 120) sts.

The easy checkerboard stitch pattern adds extra interest to the basic pullover.

Joining Sections

Joining Front Sections

Work in patt across right front section, CO 16 sts, work in patt across left front section using same yarn. At this point you can cut yarn from left front section.

Cont working in patt as established until front yoke measures same length as back yoke, ending with WS row.

Joining Front and Back Sections

Rnd 1: Knit across front sts; pm. Knit across back sts; pm (using different color to denote beg of rnd).

Rnds 2, 4, and 6: Purl.

Rnds 3 and 5: Knit.

Work even in St st (knit every round) until body measures 22 (23, 23, 24)" or 1" less than desired finished length.

Bottom Border

Rnds 1 and 3: Purl.

Rnds 2 and 4: Knit.

BO in purl.

Sleeves

With RS facing you and 24" size 7 circular needle, PU 86 (90, 94, 98) sts around armhole opening.

Rnd 1: Knit.

Rnds 2 and all even-numbered rnds through 16 (WS): Knit.

Rnds 3, 5, and 7: K4 (0, 2, 4), P6, *K6, P6, rep from * to last 4 (0, 2, 4) sts, K4 (0, 2, 4).

Rnd 9: Knit.

Rnds 11, 13, and 15: P4 (0, 2, 4) K6, *P6, K6, rep from * to last 4 (0, 2, 4) sts, P4 (0, 2, 4).

Maintaining est patt, dec 1 st at each end of next rnd and every 4th rnd thereafter until 46 (50, 54, 58) sts rem. Change to size 7 dpns when sts no longer fit on 16" circular needle.

Work even in patt until sleeve measures 18½" from beg *or* 1" less than desired finished length, ending with either rnd 2 or 10.

Change to 16" size 6 dpns and work 5 rows in garter st (knit 1 rnd, purl 1 rnd). BO in purl.

Attach yarn and with RS facing you, K24 (30, 36, 42) sts for right front; place next 36 sts onto st holder to be used later for back neck; attach 2nd ball of yarn and K24 (30, 36, 42) sts for left front.

Working both sides of front AT SAME TIME from separate skeins of yarn, cont in patt as for back, beg with row 10. Work even until front sections measure 1", ending with WS row. Inc 1 st at neck edge of each front on next row and every RS row to 34 (40, 46, 52) sts on each side, ending with WS row.

Finishing

Neck Border

Rnd 1: With RS facing you and starting at back neck edge, using 16" size 6 circular needle, PU 36 sts from st holder, PU 24 sts along left front edge, K16 sts from front holder, PU 24 sts along right front edge—100 sts total. Pm to denote beg of rnd.

Rnd 2: Purl.

Rnd 3: Knit, dec 8 sts evenly spaced around—92 sts rem.

Rnd 4: Purl.

BO in purl.

Weave in ends. Block sweater.

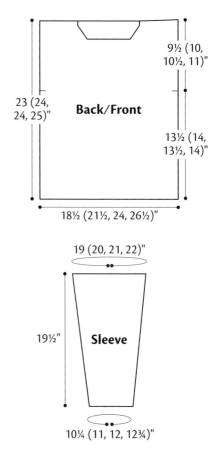

Back/Front

9½ (10, 10½, 11)"

23 (24, 24, 25)"

13½ (14, 13½, 14)"

18½ (21½, 24, 26½)"

Sleeve

19 (20, 21, 22)"

19½"

10¼ (11, 12, 12¾)"

Turnaround Vest

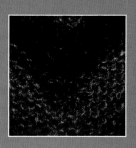

Skill level: Intermediate ◼◼◼◻

Finished bust measurement: 36 (40, 44, 48, 52)"

Finished length: 20 (20, 21, 21, 22)",
excluding point section

Materials

Yarn: 6 (7, 9, 10, 11) skeins of Silk Garden Lite from Noro
Yarns (50 g; 125 m; 45% silk/45% kid mohair/10% lamb's
wool) in color 2010 (multicolored), or approx 800 (945,
1080, 1250, 1440) yds of DK-weight yarn (3)

Needles: Size 6 straight needles and 24" and 29" size 6
circular needles or size required to obtain gauge

Notions: Stitch holders, stitch markers in various colors

Gauge: 5 sts and 9 rows = 1" in garter st

Front and Back Center Panels

CO 65 sts using straight needles.

Row 1 (RS): Knit.

Row 2: K2tog, K29, inc in next two sts, K30, K2tog tbl.

Rep rows 1 and 2 until piece measures 18 (18, 19, 19, 20)",
ending with RS row.

BO in knit on WS.

Make 2nd center panel in same manner.

Shoulder Sections

With RS facing you, using 29" circular needle and beg at
lower side edge of one center panel, PU 90 (90, 95, 95,
100) sts, CO on 10 sts for shoulder, with RS facing you
and beg at top side edge of other center panel, PU an
additional 90 (90, 95, 95, 100) sts—190 (190, 200, 200,
210) total sts.

Beg with WS row, work in garter st (knit every row) for 2
(3, 3, 4, 4)", ending with WS row. *Do not BO.*

*Because the front and back of this vest are shaped exactly the
same, it can be worn in either direction. Thus, by taking advantage
of the color range within each skein of the Noro yarn, you
can create one vest with two totally different looks.*

Side Panels

Set-up rnd: With RS facing you, K50 (50, 55, 55, 55) sts; place next 90 (90, 90, 90, 100) sts onto st holders; CO 20 (20, 30, 30, 40) sts; knit across 50 (50, 55, 55, 55) sts from 2nd side; CO 20 (20, 30, 30, 40) sts—140 (140, 170, 170, 190) total sts on needle.

Beg working side panels in the round as follows:

Rnd 1: P50 (50, 55, 55, 55) sts, pm, P20 (20, 30, 30, 40) sts, pm, P50 (50, 55, 55, 55) sts, pm, P20 (20, 30, 30, 40); pm of different color to denote beg of rnd.

Rnd 2: K2tog, *knit to 2 sts before marker, K2tog twice, rep from * twice, knit to 2 sts before end of rnd, K2tog.

Rnd 3: Purl.

Rep rnds 2 and 3 until 2 sts rem in underarm sections, ending with rnd 2.

Next rnd: Purl, stopping 1 st *before* end of rnd.

Final dec rnd: Knit last st from previous rnd and first st from this rnd tog; knit to 1 st before next marker, K2tog, pm, K2tog; knit to 1 st before next marker, K2tog; knit to end of rnd.

BO rnd: Purl to first marker. *Do not finish remainder of rnd.* Turn work to WS and use 3-needle BO to join 2 sides tog (see "Three-Needle Bind Off" on page 9).

Finishing

Armhole bands: Return sts to 24" circular needle. With RS facing you, beg at right corner of armhole opening, PU 20 (20, 30, 30, 40) sts from underarm panel, knit rem 90 (90, 90, 90, 100) armhole sts—110 (110, 120, 120, 140) total sts.

BO in purl.

Weave in ends. Block vest.

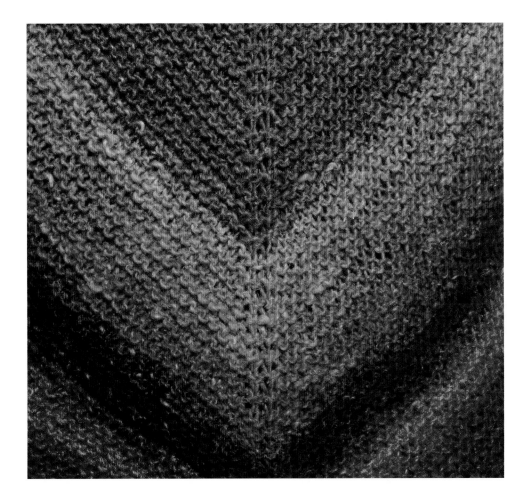

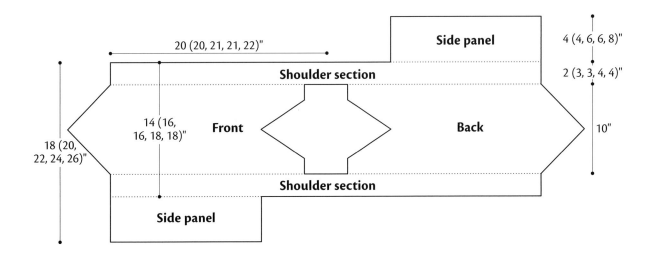

Side panel

20 (20, 21, 21, 22)"

Shoulder section

4 (4, 6, 6, 8)"

2 (3, 3, 4, 4)"

14 (16,
16, 18, 18)"

Front

Back

10"

18 (20,
22, 24, 26)"

Shoulder section

Side panel

Puff Pullover

Skill level: Intermediate ■■■□

Finished bust measurement: 35 (39, 43½, 48, 52½)"

Finished length: 21 (22, 23, 24, 25)"

Sleeve drop: 10 (10, 10½, 11, 11)"

Materials

Yarn: 11 (13, 15, 17, 20) skeins of Baby Twist from Alpaca with a Twist (1.75 oz/50 g; 110 yds; 100% baby alpaca) in color 3003 (rust heather) or approx 1200 (1400, 1600, 1850, 2100) yds of DK-weight or light worsted-weight yarn ⑶

Needles: Size 6 straight needles or circular needle or size required to obtain gauge, 16" size 5 circular needle

Notions: Stitch markers, stitch holders, scrap of smooth DK-weight or light worsted-weight yarn, size F (3.75 mm) crochet hook

Gauge

5½ sts and 7 rows = 1" in St st

Back

Using size 6 straight needles or circular needle and beg at top of back, provisionally CO 96 (108, 120, 132, 144) sts (see "Provisional Cast On" on page 7).

Row 1 (RS): Knit.

Row 2: Purl.

Rows 3, 5, and 7: *P3, K3, rep from * across row.

Rows 4, 6, and 8: Purl.

Row 9: Knit.

Row 10: Purl.

Rows 11, 13, and 15: *K3, P3, rep from * across row.

Rows 12, 14, and 16: Purl.

Rep rows 1–16 until back measures 20 (21, 22, 23, 24)" *or* 1" less than desired finished length, ending with row 2 or 10.

Bottom border: Change to size 5 circular needle. Knit 5 rows. BO in knit on WS.

Super-soft alpaca yarn makes this pullover's stitch pattern puff out.

Front

Remove provisional CO and place sts onto size 6 needle, being careful not to lose any sts (see "Removing the Chain" on page 7). With RS facing you, attach yarn and K30 (36, 39, 45, 48) sts for right front; place next 36 (36, 42, 42, 48) sts onto st holder to be used later for back neck; attach 2nd ball of yarn and attach yarn and K30 (36, 39, 42, 48) for left front. Working both sections AT SAME TIME using separate skeins of yarn, turn work and purl back.

Cont in patt as for back beg with row 3.

Work even until front sections measure 1", ending with WS row.

Inc 1 st at neck edge of each front on next row and every RS row 10 times total, ending with WS row—40 (46, 49, 55, 58) sts on each side.

Joining front sections: Work in patt across right front sts; CO 16 (16, 22, 22, 28) sts, work in patt across left front section using same yarn—96 (108, 120, 132, 144) sts. At this point you can cut the yarn from left front section.

Cont working in patt as established until front measures same length as back to start of bottom border.

Rep bottom border as for back section.

Sleeves

Starting at top of shoulder, measure 10 (10, 10½, 11, 11)" down each side of sweater and pm.

Row 1: With RS facing you and size 6 needles, PU 111 (111, 117, 123, 123) sts from between markers.

Rows 2 and all even rows through 16 (WS): Purl.

Rows 3, 5, and 7: *K3, P3, rep from * to last 3 sts, K3.

Row 9: Knit.

Rows 11, 13, and 15: *P3, K3, rep from * to last 3 sts, P3.

Maintaining patt as established, dec 1 st at each end of next row and every 4th row thereafter until you have 49 (55, 55, 61, 61) sts.

Work even in patt until sleeve measures 18 (18, 17, 17, 17)" from beg or 1" less than desired finished length, ending with row 2 or 10.

Change to 16" size 5 circular needle. Work 5 rows in garter st. BO in knit on WS.

Finishing

Neck Border

Rnd 1: With RS facing you, starting at back neck edge and using 16" size 5 circular needle, PU 36 (36, 42, 42, 48) sts from st holder; PU 24 sts along left front edge; PU 16 (16, 22, 22, 28) sts from center front CO edge, PU 24 sts along right front edge—100 (100, 112, 112, 124) sts. Pm to denote beg of rnd.

Rnd 2: Purl.

Rnd 3: Knit, dec 8 sts evenly spaced around—92 (92, 104, 104, 116) sts rem.

Rnd 4: Purl.

BO in purl.

Sew underarm and side seams. Weave in ends. Block sweater.

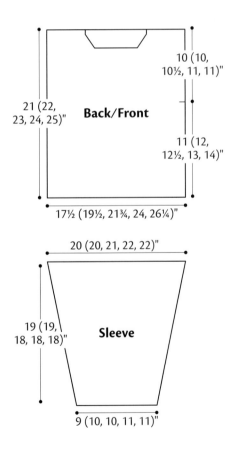

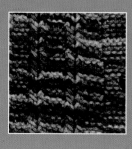

Resources

The following companies have supplied yarns and/or buttons for this book. Their generosity is greatly appreciated. For a list of shops in your area that carry the products mentioned in this book, contact these companies.

Alpaca with a Twist
4272 Evans Jacobi Rd.
Georgetown, IN 47122
www.alpacawithatwist.com

Cascade Yarns
PO Box 58168
Tukwila, WA 98138-1168
www.cascadeyarns.com

Dill Buttons of America Inc.
50 Choate Circle
Montoursville, PA 17754-9639
www.dill-buttons.com

Elsebeth Lavold
Elizabeth Austin/Knitting Fever Inc.
35 Debevoise Ave.
Roosevelt, NY 11575-0502
www.knittingfever.com

Farmhouse Yarns/Hopyard Spinnery
283 Mount Parnassus Rd.
East Haddam, CT 06423
www.farmhouseyarns.com

Interlacements
PO Box 3082
Colorado Springs, CO 80934-3082
www.interlacementsyarns.com

Koigu Wool Designs
RR #1 Williamsford
Ontario, Canada N0H 2V0
www.koigu.com

Marr Haven
772 39th St.
Allegan, MI 49010
www.marrhaven.com

Noro Yarns
Knitting Fever Inc.
35 Debevoise Ave.
Roosevelt, NY 11575-0502
www.knittingfever.com

Queensland Collection
Euroyarns/Knitting Fever Inc.
35 Debevoise Ave.
Roosevelt, NY 11575-0502
www.knittingfever.com

Shelridge Farm
RR #2 Ariss
Ontario, Canada N0B 1B0
www.shelridge.com

Skacel Collection Inc.
PO Box 88110
Seattle, WA 98138
www.skacelknitting.com

Wool in the Woods
58 Scarlet Way
Biglerville, PA 17307
www.woolinthewoods.com

Abbreviations

approx	approximately		pm	place marker
beg	begin(ning)		psso	pass slipped stitch over
BO	bind off		PU	pick up and knit
CC	contrasting color		rem	remain(ing)
ch	chain(s)		rep(s)	repeat(s)
CO	cast on		RS	right side
cont	continue		sc	single crochet
dec	decrease(ing)(s)		sl	slip
dpn(s)	double-pointed needle(s)		sm	slip marker
g	gram(s)		ssk	slip, slip, knit
inc	increase(ing)(s)		st(s)	stitch(es)
K	knit		St st	stockinette stitch
K2tog	knit 2 stitches together		tbl	through back loop(s)
M1	make 1 stitch: lift horizontal strand between the needles from front to back and place on left-hand needle; knit through back loop of stitch formed		tog	together
			WS	wrong side
			wyib	with yarn in back
MC	main color		wyif	with yarn in front
oz	ounce(s)		yd(s)	yard(s)
P	purl		YO(s)	yarn over(s)

Useful Information

Standard Yarn-Weight System

Yarn-Weight Symbol and Category Names	1 Super Fine	2 Fine	3 Light	4 Medium	5 Bulky	6 Super Bulky
Types of Yarns in Category	Sock, Fingering, Baby	Sport, Baby	DK, Light Worsted	Worsted, Afghan, Aran	Chunky, Craft, Rug	Bulky, Roving
Knit Gauge Ranges in Stockinette Stitch to 4"	27 to 32 sts	23 to 26 sts	21 to 24 sts	16 to 20 sts	12 to 15 sts	6 to 11 sts
Recommended Needle in Metric Size Range	2.25 to 3.25 mm	3.25 to 3.75 mm	3.75 to 4.5 mm	4.5 to 5.5 mm	5.5 to 8 mm	8 mm and larger
Recommended Needle in U.S. Size Range	1 to 3	3 to 5	5 to 7	7 to 9	9 to 11	11 and larger

Skill Levels

◼□□□ **Beginner:**
Projects for first-time knitters using basic knit and purl stitches. Minimal shaping.

◼◼□□ **Easy:**
Projects using basic stitches, repetitive stitch patterns, and simple color changes. Simple shaping and finishing.

◼◼◼□ **Intermediate:**
Projects using a variety of stitches, such as basic cables and lace, simple intarsia, and techniques for double-pointed needles and knitting in the round. Midlevel shaping and finishing.

Metric Conversions

m	= yds	x	0.9144
yds	= m	x	1.0936
g	= oz	x	28.35
oz	= g	x	0.0352

About the Author

A self-taught knitter who began knitting at the age of nine, Doreen L. Marquart cannot remember a time when she didn't knit. Knitting has always been a part of her life, and in 1993 she turned her passion into a business. While working at a local fabric-and-crafts store teaching various knitting classes, Doreen had become discouraged about the lack of quality yarns available. With encouragement from her husband, Gordon, and friends, she took the plunge and opened Needles 'n Pins Yarn Shoppe.

From its meager start in a converted 1½-car garage to its present 1,200-square-foot custom-built structure, Needles 'n Pins is the largest shop in its area that is devoted exclusively to the needs of knitters and crocheters. Doreen takes pride in offering quality yarns, books, and accessories that are not readily available elsewhere at an affordable price. Her excitement and passion for knitting spreads to her customers, inspiring them to try new techniques and projects. They know that at Doreen's shop, help and encouragement are always available.

Doreen is certified as a Master Knitter through both The Knitting Guild Association of America and the Canadian Guild of Knitters. *Top Down Sweaters* is her second book with Martingale & Company. Her first book, *Saturday Sweaters,* was released in September 2005. She has also done design work for Cascade Yarns and Leisure Arts.

Doreen lives in the unincorporated southeastern Wisconsin community of Richmond with her husband, Gordon.

Knitting and Crochet Titles

CROCHET

Creative Crochet *NEW!*

Crochet for Babies and Toddlers

Crochet for Tots

Crochet from the Heart

Crocheted Socks!

Crocheted Sweaters

Cute Crochet for Kids *NEW!*

The Essential Book of Crochet Techniques

Eye-Catching Crochet

First Crochet

Fun and Funky Crochet

Funky Chunky Crocheted Accessories *NEW!*

The Little Box of Crocheted Bags

The Little Box of Crocheted Hats and Scarves

The Little Box of Crocheted Ponchos and Wraps

More Crocheted Aran Sweaters

KNITTING

200 Knitted Blocks

365 Knitting Stitches a Year: Perpetual Calendar

Big Knitting

Blankets, Hats, and Booties

Dazzling Knits

Double Exposure

Everyday Style

Fair Isle Sweaters Simplified

First Knits

Fun and Funky Knitting

Funky Chunky Knitted Accessories

Handknit Style

Handknit Style II *NEW!*

Knits from the Heart

Knits, Knots, Buttons, and Bows

Knitted Shawls, Stoles, and Scarves

The Knitter's Book of Finishing Techniques

Lavish Lace

The Little Box of Knits for Baby *NEW!*

The Little Box of Knitted Ponchos and Wraps

The Little Box of Knitted Throws

The Little Box of Scarves

The Little Box of Scarves II

The Little Box of Sweaters

Modern Classics *NEW!*

Perfectly Brilliant Knits

The Pleasures of Knitting

Pursenalities

Pursenality Plus

Ribbon Style

Romantic Style

Sarah Dallas Knitting

Saturday Sweaters

Sensational Knitted Socks

Silk Knits *NEW!*

Simply Beautiful Sweaters

The Ultimate Knitted Tee

The Yarn Stash Workbook